Have Breakfast With Us
II

Wisconsin Bed and Breakfast
Homes and Historic Inns
Association's Cookbook

Have Breakfast With Us II

Copyright © 1993 by

Wisconsin Bed and Breakfast Homes
and Historic Inns Association

All rights reserved

Reproduction in whole or in part of any portion
in any form without permission is prohibited.

First Edition

Library of Congress Number 93-60707
ISBN 0-942495-28-4

This book printed in the USA
by
Palmer Publications, Inc.
Amherst, WI 54406

This book is dedicated to all our guests, who have discovered the many joys of Bed and Breakfast travelling.

Welcome . . . to our association's second cookbook, filled with breakfast treats from our members. We were delighted with the response toward our first edition and are please to offer an expanded second directory-cookbook.

We, the Wisconsin Bed and Breakfast Homes and Historic Inns Association (WBBHHIA, as it is called) look forward to greeting you when visiting our homes and country inns. The highlight of your stay is breakfast where your hosts get a chance to show off their talents by tempting you with their favorite recipes.

To make your stay memorable, you will be welcomed by friendly hospitality, comfortable beds, a relaxing atmosphere, and information about the area.

Please call any of us about the recipes or for reservation information (room rates are subject to change.) We look forward to accommodating your vacation desires.

And now . . .

Have Breakfast With Us II!

Table Of Contents

Happy Apple Dabble
Albany Guest House . . . . Albany, WI **1**

Allyn Mansion Bread
Allyn Mansion Inn . . . . Delavan, WI **3**

Cherry/Chocolate Chip Bread
Amberwood . . . . Algoma, WI **5**

Annie's Breakfast Cookies
Annie's Bed and Breakfast . . . . Madison, WI **7**

Pumpkin Muffins
Bayberry Inn, The . . . . Lake Mills **9**

German Apple Pecan Pancake
Bettinger House Bed and Breakfast . . . . Plain, WI **11**

Impossible Quiche
Birdsong Bed and Breakfast . . . . Wild Rose, WI **13**

Swiss Woods Souffle
Brandt Quirk Manor . . . . Watertown, WI **15**

Danish Pastry
Breese Waye . . . . Portage, WI **17**

Golden Delight Pancakes
Brennan Manor Bed and Breakfast . . . . Eagle River, WI **19**

Puffed Stuffed French Toast
Brick House Bed and Breakfast, The . . . . Merrill, WI **21**

Cameo Rose Carrot Cake (or Muffins)
Cameo Rose Bed and Breakfast . . . . Belleville, WI **23**

Candlewick Strawberry Bread
Candlewick Inn . . . . Merrill, WI **25**

Wake-Up Cake
Chase on the Hill Bed and Breakfast . . . . Milton, WI **27**

Good Morning Muffins
Chelsea Rose . . . . Kewaunee, WI **29**

Baked French Toast
Country Woods . . . . Ellison Bay, WI **31**

Irresistible Orange Date Muffins . . . A Canadian Favorite
Courthouse Square Bed and Breakfast . . . . Crandon, WI **33**

v

Company Eggs and Ham
    Crystal River Bed and Breakfast .... Waupaca, WI **35**

Eggs Goldenrod
    Cunningham House, The .... Platteville, WI **37**

Swiss Turkey Quiche
    Dering House .... Columbus, WI **39**

Morning Pumpkin Coffeecake
    Dreams of Yesteryear Bed and Breakfast ...... Stevens Point, WI **41**

Cherry-Cream Cheese Coffeecake
    East Highland Bed and Breakfast .... Phillips, WI **43**

Baked Egg and Cheese Casserole
    Fargo Mansion Inn, The .... Lake Mills, WI **45**

Potato Pancakes
    Ferg Haus Inn .... Manawa, WI **47**

Stromboli
    Forgotten Tymes .... Siren, WI **49**

Walt's Granola
    French Country Inn of Ephraim .... Ephraim, WI **51**

Criss-Cross Coffeecake
    "Gables", The .... Kewaunee, WI **53**

Swedish Pears
    Gray Goose Bed and Breakfast, The .... Sturgeon Bay, WI **55**

Springtime Rhubarb Pie . . . Wisconsin Style
    Greystone Farm's Bed and Breakfast .... East Troy, WI **57**

Carol's Harrisburg Breakfast Casserole
    Harrisburg Inn Bed and Breakfast .... Maiden Rock, WI **59**

Oven Puffed French Toast
    Hill Street Bed and Breakfast .... Spring Green, WI **61**

Oatmeal Pancakes
    Hillcrest Inn and Carriage House .... Burlington, WI **63**

Peach French Toast Supreme
    Historic Bennett House .... Wisconsin Dells, WI **65**

Pecan Twist Rolls
    Inn, The .... Montreal, WI **67**

Rarebit Au Gratin
    Inn at Grady's Farm .... Portage, WI **69**

Spiced Cranberry Nut Muffins
Inn at Pinewood, The . . . . Eagle River, WI **71**

Danebod Pancakes
Jefferson-Day House . . . . Hudson, WI **73**

Bertie's Pineapple Breakfast Rolls
Jeremiah Mabie Bed and Breakfast . . . . Delavan, WI **75**

Pecan Horns
Johnson Inn . . . . Plainfield, WI **77**

Oatmeal Raspberry Bar Cookies
Journey's End . . . . Amherst, WI **79**

Just-N-Trails Sinful Muffins
Just-N-Trails Bed and Breakfast . . . . Sparta, WI **81**

Country Breakfast Casserole
Knollwood House Bed and Breakfast . . . . River Falls, WI **83**

Elegant Egg Puff
Kraemer House Bed and Breakfast, The . . . . Plain, WI **85**

6-Week Bran Muffins
Krupp Farm Homestead, The . . . . New Holstein, WI **87**

Camp of the Woods Bread Pudding
Lambs Inn Bed and Breakfast . . . . Richland Center, WI **89**

Great Grandma's Drop Doughnuts
Lumberman's Mansion Inn . . . . Hayward, WI **91**

German Farm Breakfast
Martha's Ethnic Bed and Breakfast . . . . Westfield, WI **93**

Raspberry Stuffed French Toast
Middleton Beach Inn, The . . . . Middleton, WI **95**

Norwegian Sour Cream Waffles with Apple Pecan Topping
Mustard Seed Bed and Breakfast, The . . . . Hayward, WI **97**

Marion's Danish Pastry
Nash House—A Bed and Breakfast, The . . . . . Wisconsin Rapids, WI **99**

Pam's Southwestern Spicy Quiche
Night Heron, The . . . . Cambridge-Rockdale, WI **101**

Black Walnut Fudge Waffles
Oak Hill Manor . . . . Albany, WI **103**

Wild Blueberry Scones with Blueberry Sauce
Old Rittenhouse Inn . . . . Bayfield, WI **105**

Blueberry Buttermilk Muffins
  Parkview Bed and Breakfast . . . . Reedsburg, WI **107**

Feta Vegie Quiche with Rolled Oat and Wheat Germ Crust
  Pederson Victorian Bed and Breakfast . . . . . . Lake Geneva, WI **109**

Cherry-Berry Meringue Shortcakes
  Phipps Inn . . . . Hudson, WI **111**

Potato Broccoli Quiche
  Pinehaven Bed and Breakfast . . . . Baraboo, WI **113**

Honey Baked French Toast
  Pleasant Lake Inn . . . . Osceola, WI **115**

Grandma's Morning Muffins
  Port Washington, Inn . . . . Port Washington, WI **117**

Queen Anne's Crepes Asparagus Cordon Bleu
  Queen Anne Bed and Breakfast, The . . . . Appleton, WI **119**

Baked German Apple Pancake
  Red Forest Bed and Breakfast . . . . Two Rivers, WI **121**

Fiesta River Terrace
  River Terrace Bed and Breakfast . . . . Kiel, WI **123**

Grandmother's Famous Cranberry Bread
  Rose Ivy Inn . . . . Waupun, WI **125**

Scofield House Egg and Sausage Strata
  Scofield House Bed and Breakfast, The . . . . . . Sturgeon Bay **127**

Patty's Fireside Pumpkin Bread
  Spider Lake Lodge Bed and Breakfast . . . . Hayward, WI **129**

Golden Treat
  Sugar River Inn Bed and Breakfast . . . . Albany, WI **131**

Picante Sauce
  Summit Farm Bed and Breakfast . . . . Hammond, WI **133**

Whole Wheat Buttermilk Waffles
  Swallow's Nest Bed and Breakfast, The . . . . . Lake Delton, WI **135**

Spring Muffins
  Taylor House . . . . Iola, WI **137**

Spinach Pie
  Timm's Hill Bed and Breakfast . . . . Ogema, WI **139**

Plum Conserve
  Trillium . . . . La Farge, WI **141**

English Steamed Cranberry Pudding with Hard Sauce
   Trillium Woods Bed and Breakfast . . . . River Falls, WI **143**

Pears with Custard Sauce
   Ty-Bach . . . . Lac du Flambeau, WI **145**

Kay's Blueberry Buckle
   Victorian Garden Bed and Breakfast . . . . Monroe, WI **147**

Overnight Caramel French Toast
   Victoria-On-Main Bed and Breakfast . . . . Whitewater, WI **149**

Frosti Crepes
   Victorian Swan on Water . . . . Stevens Point, WI **151**

Elegant Eggs Florentine
   Victorian Treasure Bed and Breakfast Inn . . . . Lodi, WI **153**

Italian Sausage Breakfast Casserole
   Whistling Swan, The . . . . Fish Creek, WI **155**

Sour Cream Cherry Pancakes
   Whitefish Bay Farm . . . . Sturgeon Bay, WI **157**

Poppy Seed Bread
   White Shutters, The . . . . Lomira, WI **159**

Crepe Suzette
   Wolf River Lodge . . . . White Lake, WI **161**

Baked Stuffed Pears
   Wooden Heart Inn, The . . . . Sister Bay, WI **163**

Chocolate Tea Bread
   Yankee Hill Bed and Breakfast . . . . Plymouth, WI **165**

Bab's Philly Cinnamon Buns
   Ye Olde Manor House Bed and Breakfast . . . . . . Elkhorn, WI **167**

Albany, p. 1, 103, 131
Algoma, p. 5
Amherst, p. 79
Appleton, p. 119
Baraboo, p. 113
Bayfield, p. 105
Belleville, p. 23
Burlington, p. 63
Cambridge-Rockdale, p. 101
Columbus, p. 39
Crandon, p. 33
Delavan, p. 3, 75
Eagle River, p. 19, 71
East Troy, p. 57
Elkhorn, p. 167
Ellison Bay, p. 31
Ephraim, p. 51
Fish Creek, p. 155
Hammond, p. 133
Hayward, p. 91, 97, 129
Hudson, p. 73, 111
Iola, p. 137
Kewaunee, p. 29, 53
Kiel, p. 123
La Farge, p. 141
Lac du Flambeau, p. 145
Lake Delton, p. 135
Lake Geneva, p. 109
Lake Mills, p. 9, 45
Lodi, p. 153
Lomira, p. 159
Madison, p. 7
Maiden Rock, p. 59
Manawa, p. 47
Merrill, p. 21, 25

Middleton, p. 95
Milton, p. 27
Monroe, p. 147
Montreal, p. 67
New Holstein, p. 87
Ogema, p. 139
Osceola, p. 115
Phillips, p. 43
Plain, p. 11, 85
Plainfield, p. 77
Platteville, p. 37
Plymouth, p. 165
Port Washington, p. 117
Portage, p. 17, 69
Reedsburg, p. 107
Richland Center, p. 89
River Falls, p. 83, 143
Siren, p. 49
Sister Bay, p. 163
Sparta, p. 81
Spring Green, p. 61
Stevens Point, p. 41, 151
Sturgeon Bay, p. 55, 127, 157
Two Rivers, p. 121
Watertown, p. 15
Waupaca, p. 35
Waupun, p. 125
Westfield, p. 93
White Lake, p. 161
Whitewater, p. 149
Wild Rose, p. 13
Wisconsin Dells, p. 65
Wisconsin Rapids, p. 99

Bayfield
Montreal
Hayward
Lac du Flambeau
Siren
Eagle River
Phillips
Crandon
Ellison Bay
Osceola
Ogema
Fish Creek
Sister Bay
Ephraim
Merrill
Hudson
White Lake
Sturgeon Bay
Hammond
River Falls
Stevens Point
Iola
Algoma
Wisconsin Rapids
Manawa
Kewaunee
Maiden Rock
Amherst
Plainfield
Appleton
Two Rivers
Wild Rose
New Holstein
Sparta
Westfield
Kiel
Plymouth
La Farge
Lake Delton
Wisconsin Dells
Waupun
Reedsburg
Portage
Lomira
Port Washington
Baraboo
Columbus
Richland Center
Plain
Lodi
Watertown
Spring Green
Middleton
Lake Mills
Madison
Cambridge-Rockdale
Belleville
Whitewater
East Troy
Platteville
Milton
Burlington
Albany
Delavan
Elkhorn
Monroe
Lake Geneva

Albany Guest House

405 S. Mill Street, Albany, WI 53502
608•862•3636

Hosts: Bob and Sally Braem

The restored 1908 three story home is made of several types of unique decorative concrete blocks placed in a most interesting design. The gleaming wood floors support king and queen beds in air conditioned rooms, private baths, Oriental carpets.

The spacious red-tiled, beam-ceilinged foyer with open oak staircase leads you to your room. Perhaps you'll choose the Master Bedroom for the wood-burning fireplace, or the Rose Room to enjoy our daughter's stained glass talents. Gardens and houseplants abound allowing you to enjoy the unusual Asiatic or day lilies, or maybe you'll be lucky enough to see an orchid blooming.

Try home-made wild fruit syrups, jellies or jams with the specialty breads and pancakes served with the hearty full breakfast. Then get a little exercise by biking or hiking the Sugar River Trail, or enjoy an easy canoe or tube ride down the gentle river.

Visit "Fannie's Amish Store" for her bakery items made each first Saturday of the month or get bulk foods and quilts anytime. New Glarus, "America's Little Switzerland" is an easy 15 mile ride by car or bike where you can sample Swiss cuisine or visit museums or festivals.

Happy Apple Dabble

6-8 servings

Ingredients:

4 cups chopped apple, leaving about half the skin on
1/2 cup maple syrup, or maple flavored syrup
3 tablespoons frozen apple juice concentrate
1/2 cup raisins
Sprinkling of cinnamon

1 cup 100% Bran
1/2 cup quick rolled oats
3 tablespoons flour
3 tablespoons brown sugar
4 tablespoons oil (I prefer canola oil)
1 cup broken Shredded Wheat (optional)
Dollops of vanilla low/no fat yogurt

Procedure:

Lightly grease microwavable or oven safe dish, about 7" x 11", or 6-8 custard cups. Mix syrup and apple juice concentrate together in bowl, add apples and raisins—toss to coat. Put into baking container or custard cups. Sprinkle with cinnamon. In the original bowl, mix next 5 ingredients; distribute evenly over apple mix. Add broken shredded wheat for topping if desired.

Bake in microwave uncovered about 6 minutes, or about 1 minute per cup. In conventional oven, bake about 30 minutes.

I serve it warm with dollop of vanilla yogurt. It's good cold too.

Rates at the Albany Guest House range from $50-$75 per night, which include a full breakfast.

Allyn Mansion Inn

511 E. Walworth Avenue, Delavan, WI 53115
414•728•9090

Hosts: Joe Johnson and Ron Markwell

Nine years of intensive restoration effort and an exhaustive search for authentic period appointments has brought the Allyn Mansion much critical acclaim. 1992 recipient of the nation's most prestigious historic preservation award, the Grand Prize of the National Trust's Great American Home Awards, the Allyn Mansion is a "traditional" B&Ber's must!

Allyn Mansion Bread

Ingredients:

1 cup cracked wheat
2 cups water
2 tablespoons molasses
1 tablespoon honey
1 tablespoon salt
1 stick butter or margarine
    (I use Country Crock. It cooks like butter but is better for you.)
1 cup buttermilk
1/2 cup warm water
2 tablespoons yeast (two packages)
1 teaspoon sugar
6 cups (approximately) white flour

Procedure:

Simmer for 10 minutes the cracked wheat in the 2 cups of water. Add, while simmering, the molasses, honey, salt and butter (or margarine).
Remove from heat and add the buttermilk. Let cool to working temperature.
In a separate bowl, mix the warm water, yeast and sugar.
When yeast is dissolved and has puffed up, add to cracked wheat mixture. Add white flour until you can't stir in anymore. Turn onto floured board and knead until the dough quits fighting back which will take about 10 minutes. Let rise, covered with damp towel, in greased bowl twice before forming into 2 or 3 loaves. Let rise (covered) again and bake about 30 minutes at 400°.

I buy yeast at a health food store. It is better and cheaper.
This bread freezes well. I use heavy plastic bags which I also get at a health food store.

Rates at the Allyn Mansion Inn range from $45-$85, which include a full breakfast.

Amberwood

N7136 Hwy 42, Lakeshore Drive, Algoma, WI 54201
414•487•3471

Hosts: Jan and George

At Amberwood Inn, George and Jan serve breakfast in the sunny breakfast room surrounded by stained glass windows and overlooking the beauty of the Lake Michigan shore.

Breakfast is always large and hearty with many southwestern dishes featured. Homemade bread/cinnamon rolls abound. Chocolate (the first major food group) is often included in the fare at Amberwood. Great guests, good times and luxury surroundings make your stay memorable.

Amberwood features large, private suites. Each suite has a private bath (some with a whirlpool tub), and private deck opening to the beach. Most suites offer a wet bar or refrigerator. Amberwood is nestled on 2½ acres of private woods, with 300 feet of Lake Michigan beach—secluded, romantic, private and luxurious.

Welcome to Amberwood, where country charm meets waterfront luxury.

Cherry/Chocolate Chip Bread

2 loaves

Ingredients:

3 eggs
1 cup sugar
1 1/4 cups flour
2 teaspoons baking powder
2 cups chocolate chips
1 cup of each:
Walnuts or pecans
Chopped maraschino cherries (with juice)
Chopped dates

Procedure:

Mix all ingredients together. Pour into two greased loaf pans. Bake at 250° for 1 1/2 hours. (If baking four or more cook 2 1/2 to 3 hours.) Remove from pans. Cool and slice. Wrap in foil and refrigerate; will keep 2 weeks.

Rates at the Amberwood range from $55-$75 with a full breakfast included.

Annie's Bed and Breakfast

2117 Sheridan Drive, Madison, WI 53704
608•244•2224

Hosts: Anne and Larry Stuart

Opened as Madison's first bed and breakfast in April of 1985, Annie's is a rustic cedar shake home in a quiet neighborhood overlooking a beautiful valley view of Warner Park, a block away from the eastern shore of Lake Mendota. The two guest suites (each consisting of two bedrooms and a private bath) have in-room tv/vcr's and a large selection of movies. Thick terrycloth robes enable guests to get to the woodland whirlpool room for a soothing end to their day.

Stroll nature paths to the lake where you can swim, go fishing, or enjoy a quiet picnic lunch. Play tennis at the shaded park courts, or bike/hike to the Governor's Mansion or Island Nature Conservancy close-by. Look through the guest book for comments from guests through the years in order to sense the true flavor of this most unusual bed and breakfast. Many guests have become friends, returning to be refreshed by the immense quiet and tranquility of the beautiful setting, and renew acquaintances once again. Annie's is open year-round and a beautiful brochure is yours for the asking!

Annie's Breakfast Cookies

makes 24

Ingredients:

3 1/2 cups milk
4 cups old fashioned oats
6 tablespoons vegetable oil
6 beaten eggs (large)
1 cup raisins
4 tablespoons brown sugar
1 tablespoon baking powder
1/2 teaspoon salt
1 1/2 cups chopped fruit
    (your choice of apples, cranberries, bananas)
1 cup chopped nuts

Procedure:

    Combine milk, oil, beaten eggs, raisins. Add oats and soak for five minutes. Stir in dry ingredients. Add fruit and nuts last. Using a 1/4 cup measure, spread this amount of batter on oiled griddle (set at no more than 325° to avoid over-browning). Turn once. Do not allow to brown but rather just cook through. These pancakes will be thick and hearty. They are usually served with maple syrup, often some fresh fruit, a generous heap of country bacon sausages, and a tall frosty glass of fresh orange juice at the side.

    This is just a sample of the hearty country breakfasts that have become the trademark of Annie's. Along with the supreme peace and tranquility of the setting, and warm hospitality offered, guests have been returning to this bed and breakfast for many years. . . .

Rates at Annie's range from $75-$100 for double occupancy, and include a full breakfast.

The Bayberry Inn

265 S. Main Street, Lake Mills, WI 53551
414•648•3654

Hosts: Barry Luce and Tom Boycks

Casual country comfort in a turn of the century renovated hotel. Large, airy rooms done in country pastels. Ideal for families or large groups. Close to Rock Lake, Aztalan State Park, and Glacial Drumlin Bike Trail. Group rates available.

Pumpkin Muffins

yields 12

Ingredients:

1 1/2 cups flour
1/2 cup sugar
2 teaspoons baking powder
1/2 teaspoon salt
1/2 teaspoon cinnamon
1/2 teaspoon nutmeg
1/2 cup of milk
1/2 cup canned pumpkin
1/4 cup butter, melted (1/2 stick)
1 egg

Procedure:

    Mix all ingredients together. Stir until well blended. Be careful not to overmix. Spoon batter into greased muffin pan. Sprinkle sugar over batter in each cup. Bake at 400° for 18-20 minutes. Remove and serve warm.

Rates range from $45-$55 per night and include a continental breakfast.

Bettinger House Bed and Breakfast

855 Wachter Avenue, Plain, WI 53577
608•546•2951

Hosts: Jim and Marie Neider

Since Germany's early days, heart and hearth have gone together with this name. If your last name was Bettinger, your birth place was Bettingen.

The Bettinger House, in Plain, WI, has a history of being home to an extended family. In the early 1900's, Philip and Elizabeth Bettinger hosted traveling entertainers and medicine peddlers. Later, Elizabeth took in roomers.

Today, Marie and Jim Nieder invite travelers into the home and lives of Marie's ancestral family. Each room is named for a family member. You can read about their lives, pour over family photos, or coax Marie to share memories.

Soon you too will be an extended member of the Bettinger family.

German Apple Pecan Pancake

4 servings

Ingredients:

1/4 cup butter
2 apples, peeled, cored, and thinly sliced
3 eggs
1/2 cup milk
1/2 cup all-purpose flour
1/4 cup sugar
1/2 teaspoon cinnamon
1/2 cup pecans

Procedure:

In a heavy 10" ovenproof skillet, heat 2 tablespoons of butter. Add apples and cook over medium heat until apples are just tender, stirring occasionally.

Batter—in a blender combine eggs, milk, flour, 1/4 teaspoon salt. Cover and blend mixture until it's smooth. Pour the pancake batter over the apples in the skillet. Sprinkle pecans over top. Bake at 375° uncovered for 18 minutes or until puffy and golden.

Dot the puff pancake with the remaining butter and sprinkle with the sugar and cinnamon. Return to oven and bake 2 minutes more. Serve pancake immediately.

Rates at the Bettinger House range from $45-$60, which include a full breakfast.

Birdsong Bed and Breakfast

930 East County A, Wild Rose, WI 54984-0391
414•622•3770

Hosts: Walter and Sallyann Bouwens

Watching our winged friends at close proximity while enjoying a delicious breakfast is a delightful beginning for each new day at Birdsong Bed and Breakfast. Seasonal visitors to our many feeding stations as well as the beautiful plumage of permanent residents wait to be identified and marveled over by guests! Seventy-five acres are available for nature walking and private contemplation.

The guest rooms are large and roomy for one or two occupants. Depending on individual interests, there is a generous parlor for reading, watching television or movies on the VCR. We also have wonderful room for family reunions, wedding receptions, and meetings of all kinds.

Original art of various styles can be enjoyed throughout the home. With an evening fire in the fireplace, and someone special to sit with, the library offers volumes of great diversity from the ridiculous to the sublime! Books are distributed throughout our home, and it is a joy to see all ages opting for books in lieu of television.

Impossible Quiche

6-8 servings

Ingredients:

3 eggs
1/2 cup Bisquick
1/2 cup melted butter
1 1/2 cups milk
1/4 teaspoon salt
Dash pepper
1 cup shredded Swiss cheese
1/2 cup ham or bacon, cut in small pieces

Procedure:

Place all ingredients—except cheese and meat—in blender and mix for a few seconds to blend well.

Pour into greased 9" pie pan or 8" x 8" Pyrex square dish.

Sprinkle cheese and meat over top and push gently below the surface with back of spoon.

Bake at 350° for 45 minutes.

Allow to set 10 minutes before cutting.

Note: I substitute asparagus (canned) in lieu of meat for vegetarian guests. Also, can be served warm, not hot, if desired.

We feel so grateful to have Birdsong to offer as a refreshing place to visit.

Rates at the Birdsong Bed and Breakfast range from $55-$125 per night including a full breakfast.

Brandt Quirk Manor

410 South Fourth Street, Watertown, WI 53094
414•261•7917

Hosts: Wayne and Elda Zuleger

Frederick Brandt constructed this Greek revival home in 1875. It has been restored to the elegance and grandure of this bygone era.

The manor features Ionic pillars, inside and out, stained glass windows, marble sinks, marble and ceramic fireplaces, parquet flooring, and decorative plaster accents. Guests are welcome to relax in either of the living rooms or dining areas.

The manor has four guest rooms, two with adjoining sitting areas. One has a private bath the other three share a full and half bath. The manor is furnished with many period antiques.

Come; relax. Enjoy the hospitality, tour the Octagon House, and First Kindergarten. Walk the river front boardwalk or view many of the fine historical homes of Watertown.

Swiss Woods Souffle

8 servings

Ingredients:

6-8 slices of bread, cut in pieces
5 eggs
2 cups of milk, divided 1 1/2 cups and 1/2 cup
1/4 teaspoon salt
1/4 teaspoon pepper
1/2 teaspoon dry mustard
1 pound bulk pork sausage, browned and drained
1 can of condensed cream of mushroom soup
1 cup of mixed Guyere and Emmenthaler cheese (Aged Swiss may be substituted)

Procedure:

Distribute bread pieces evenly over the bottom of a greased 9" x 13" pan. Mix eggs with 1 1/2 cup milk and spices. Pour over bread and let stand 15 minutes.
Spread meat over top.
Combine soup, 1/2 cup milk and cheeses. Spread on top.
Bake at 350° for 45 minutes. Let stand 5 minutes before cutting.
This can be made the night before.

Rates at the Brandt Quirk Manor range from $55-$75, including a full breakfast.

Breese Waye

816 MacFarlane Road, Portage, WI 53901
608•742•5281

Hosts: Keith and Gretchen Sprecher

Circa 1880.

When guests step in the door they "ooh & aah" over reminders of grandma's house. "I remember Gram had one just like that in her living room."

Unwind as you step back into this historical Victorian home.

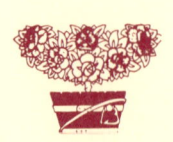

Danish Pastry

24 - 1" slices

Ingredients:

CRUST:
1 cup flour
1/2 cup butter
2 tablespoons water

TOPPING:
1/2 cup butter
1 cup water
1 teaspoon vanilla
1 cup flour
3 eggs

Procedure:

CRUST:
Mix as pie crust, roll in ball and divide in half. *Pat into 2 long strips 12" x 3", 1/4-inch thick on a large cookie sheet.
*When patting out the crust, dip hands under warm running water frequently.

TOPPING:
Bring water and butter to a boil, add vanilla, remove from heat and add flour all at one time. Beat fast until smooth, then add 1 egg at a time, beating until smooth after each egg.

Spread on top of the two 12" x 3" strips. Bake one hour at 350°. Frost when cool, with your favorite frosting recipe.

Rates at the Breese Waye range from $45-$55, which include a full breakfast.

Brennan Manor Bed and Breakfast

1079 Everett Road, Eagle River, WI 54521
715•479•7353

Hosts: Robert and Connie Lawton

This lakeside English Tudor evokes images of King Arthur with its suit of armor, arched windows, hand-hewn woodwork and 30-foot stone fireplace.

"When we bought this home, its floor plan and old world charm seemed conducive to a bed and breakfast," say innkeepers Connie and Bob Lawton.

You'll stay in one of four antique-decorated rooms (private baths) that open onto a balcony overlooking the Great Room. There, wintertime guests gather to sip hot chocolate and munch popcorn after cross-country skiing in the Nicolet National Forest or snowmobiling on 500 miles of trails.

Situated on the largest freshwater chain of lakes in the world, the inn's frontage includes a boathouse and piers for warm-weather fun. A four bedroom guest house is also available.

Golden Delight Pancakes

24 - 3" pancakes

Ingredients:

1 cup cream style cottage cheese
6 eggs
1/2 cup sifted flour
1/4 cup oil
1/4 cup milk
1/2 teaspoon vanilla

Procedure:

Put all ingredients into blender. Blend at high speed 1 minute, stopping to stir once. Cook on hot griddle in desired sizes.
Pancakes may be frozen; reheated in toaster.

Rates at the Brennan Manor Bed and Breakfast range from $69-$89. Rates include a full breakfast.

The Brick House Bed and Breakfast

108 S. Cleveland Street, Merrill, WI 54452
715•536•3230

Hosts: Kris and Randy Ullmer

In 1915, P.C. Daly, the grandfather of actress Tyne Daly ("Cagney and Lacey"), built the Prairie style home which is now The Brick House Bed and Breakfast. Handsome wood and the comfortable simplicity of mission furnishings invite relaxation.

Merrill, known as the "City of Parks" with nine city parks and one state park, is perfect for walking and biking . . . away from the crowds. A few steps from our front door the Wisconsin River flows: observe wildlife or wet a fishing line during a lazy canoe ride. Abundant snowfall transforms the area into a white winter playground with miles of groomed cross-country trails.

Puffed Stuffed French Toast

serves 4-6

Ingredients:

1 loaf firm/dense sour dough bread
8 ounce cream cheese
1/2 cup chopped walnuts
10 eggs
1 1/2 cups half-n-half
1/4 cup maple syrup
8 tablespoons butter (melted)
1 teaspoon vanilla

Procedure:

Remove crust and tear bread into small pieces. Layer half in greased 9" x 11" baking dish. Place sliced cream cheese on bread; sprinkle with chopped nuts. Cover with remaining bread.
Beat together the eggs, half-n-half, syrup and vanilla; stir in butter. Pour mixture over the bread; refrigerate overnight, covered.
Bake uncovered at 350° for 1 hour (or more, until quite brown). Let rest 5 minutes before serving.
Serve with warm Wisconsin pure maple syrup or fruit syrup.

Before it's even tasted, the sight of Puffed Stuffed French Toast elicits oohs and aahs . . . conversation then slows as the rich creation is savored. At The Brick House, Puffed Stuffed French Toast is preceded by fresh fruits and accompanied by locally produced maple syrup, thinly sliced honey ham, juice and gourmet coffee.

Rates at The Brick House range from $40-$60, and include a full breakfast.

Cameo Rose Bed and Breakfast

1090 Henry & Severson Junction, Belleville, WI 53508
608•424•6340

Hosts: Dawn and Gary Bahr

Welcome to the Cameo Rose—a unique country experience between Madison and New Glarus, where old-fashioned Victorian charm blends with modern comforts and convenience. Amidst a pristine setting of 120 wooded acres, trails meander along the hillsides past glacier-carved rock formations, miles of berry bushes and wild flowers. Inside, Dawn's love of antique china, vintage lace and roses are not for those who prefer a spartan look. Guest rooms feature private baths, king and queen size beds and antique dressers.

At check-in, guests are often greeted by the aroma of freshly baked cookies, bars or a favorite—Dawn's carrot cake. This dessert has been our most requested recipe and many guests claim it's the best they've had!

Cameo Rose Carrot Cake (or Muffins)

9" x 13" pan or about 24 muffins

Ingredients:

CAKE:
2 cups sugar
1 1/2 cups oil
4 eggs
1 cup walnuts
3 cups grated carrots
2 cups flour
1 teaspoon salt
2 teaspoons soda
3 tablespoons cinnamon
1/2 teaspoon nutmeg

ICING:
1 pound powdered sugar
3/4 stick of butter
2 teaspoons vanilla
8 ounces cream cheese (softened)
1/2 cup chopped walnuts

Procedure:

    Grate carrots, chop nuts and set aside. Mix sugar, oil and eggs; beat well. Sift dry ingredients and mix with eggs, add carrots and nuts. Bake at 350° for 35-40 minutes (for cake) or 20-25 minutes for muffins. Turn off oven and leave in for 5-10 minutes.
    For icing: Soften butter and cream cheese and cream together with powdered sugar and vanilla. Sprinkle nuts on top of iced cake.

Note: For muffins, I add about 1/4 cup hot milk to the icing and drizzle over the top. Sprinkle with nuts if desired. Un-iced cake and muffins freeze well.

Rates at the Cameo Rose are $59-$89 per night, which include a full breakfast.

Candlewick Inn

700 West Main Street, Merrill, WI 54452
1•800•382•4376, 715•536•7744

Host: Dan Staniak

Warm, romantic and elegant, this 1883 lumber baron's mansion welcomes you. Fully restored to its original beauty and appointed with fine antiques and period furnishings.

Sip your favorite beverage while relaxing with your favorite person in front of one of our cozy, crackling fireplaces or on the spacious wicker-filled screened porch.

Candlewick Strawberry Bread

1 - 5" x 9" loaf

Ingredients:

1 cup sugar
1 1/2 cups flour
1 1/2 teaspoons cinnamon
1/2 teaspoon baking soda
1/4 teaspoon salt
2/3 cup sliced almonds
2 eggs
1/2 cup cooking oil
10 ounces strawberries, sliced

Procedure:

    Preheat oven to 350°. Grease and flour a 5" x 9" loaf pan.
    Mix together first six ingredients. Add eggs and oil and blend together. Fold in berries.
    Put mixture in prepared pan and bake at 350° from 1 hour to 1 hour and 10 minutes.
    Remove from pan and cool on wire rack.

Rates at the Candlewick Bed and Breakfast Inn range from $50-$95, which include a full breakfast.

Chase on the Hill Bed and Breakfast

3928 N. State Road 26, Milton, WI 53563
608•868•6646

Host: Michael Chase

You are invited to kick off your shoes and enjoy the charm and hospitality of Chase on the Hill, a cozy farmhouse built in 1836. Four comfortable guest rooms are filled with fresh air and sunshine to provide an ideal atmosphere for peace and relaxation. The master bedroom features skylights, queen bed and a private bathroom.

Chase on the Hill is easily accessible from Madison, Milwaukee, and Chicago. Innkeeper Michael Chase, a professional actor, welcomes you!

Wake-up Cake

10 servings

Ingredients:

3/4 cup peanut butter
3/4 cup brown sugar
1/3 cup butter, softened
2 eggs
1 teaspoon vanilla
3/4 cup mashed bananas
1 1/2 cups quick oats
3/4 cup flour
1 teaspoon baking soda

Procedure:

In large bowl combine peanut butter, brown sugar, and butter, beating until light and fluffy. Beat in eggs and vanilla, then stir in bananas.

Mix oats, flour and baking soda. Stir into the above banana mixture. Spread into a greased 9" x 13" baking pan. Bake at 350° for 25-30 minutes. Cool on wire rack.

Rates at Chase on the Hill range from $40-$55 per night, which include a full breakfast.

Chelsea Rose

908 Milwaukee Street, Kewaunee, WI 54216
414•388•2012

Hosts: Gary and Cindy Rose

Enjoy the personal service our small inn provides.

Mornings you will awaken to the aromas of fresh brewed coffee and a plenty-full breakfast.

Evenings, your tastebuds will be tempted with home baked cookies—the cookie jar is always within reach.

Your days will be filled with walks along the Lake Michigan shores, stroll through our Historic District, or a day trip to nearby Door County.

New memories await you. . . .

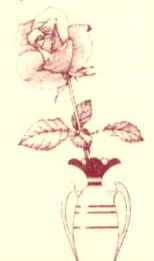

Good Morning Muffins

Yield: 12 regular or 48 mini

Ingredients:

1 large egg
3/4 cup packed brown sugar
1 1/3 cups mashed ripe bananas
1/2 cup raisins or walnuts
1/3 cup vegetable oil
1 teaspoon vanilla extract
3/4 cup all-purpose flour
3/4 cup whole wheat flour
1/2 cup oat bran
2 teaspoons baking powder
1/2 teaspoon baking soda
1 teaspoon cinnamon
1/4 teaspoon salt

Procedure:

Preheat oven to 375°. Prepare muffin tins. Beat together egg and sugar in a medium size bowl. When smooth, add bananas, raisins or walnuts, oil and vanilla.

In a separate bowl, mix flours, bran, baking powder and soda, cinnamon and salt.

Add banana mixture. Fold with a wooden spoon or spatula until dry ingredients are just moistened. Do not overmix.

Spoon batter into tins. Bake for 15-25 minutes or until brown and springy to the touch. Remove from tins and cool on rack. Serve warm.

Tastes wonderful with Honey Butter.

Rates at the Chelsea Rose Bed and Breakfast are $50, which include a full breakfast.

Country Woods

520 Europe Lake Road, Ellison Bay, WI 54210
414•854•5706

Hosts: Cheryl and Carl Carlson

Nature's delight among the private woodlands and stone gardens at Europe Lake. Canoes available. Breakfast served on sundeck when weather is warm and sunny.
Waterfront cottages and four Bed & Breakfast guest rooms for the traveler to enjoy a quiet way of life . . . yet five minutes from shops, galleries, fish boils, and the Washington Island Ferry.
Discover the unique Newport State Park and Europe Lake area with hiking, biking and canoeing.
Enjoy your Door County vacation with us . . .

Baked French Toast

6-8 servings

Ingredients:

1 baquette French bread, cut in 1-inch slices
6 large eggs
1 1/2 cups milk
1 cup cream
1 teaspoon vanilla extract
1/4 teaspoon ground cinnamon
1/4 teaspoon ground nutmeg
1/4 cup butter
1/2 cup firmly packed light brown sugar
1/2 cup sliced almonds
1 tablespoon light corn syrup
Maple syrup

Procedure:

    Butter 9" x 13" pan. Arrange bread slices (they may overlap) to fill pan. In a medium bowl combine eggs, milk, cream, vanilla, cinnamon and nutmeg. Mix well and pour over bread slices. Cover and refrigerate overnight.
    Next day: Preheat oven to 350°. In a small bowl, add butter, sugar and corn syrup. Mix well and spread evenly over bread. Sprinkle with almonds evenly. Bake for 40 minutes, or until puffed and golden. Serve with maple syrup.

Rates at the Country Woods Bed and Breakfast range from $65-$85, which include a full breakfast.

Courthouse Square Bed and Breakfast

210 East Polk Street, Crandon, WI 54465
715•478•2549

Hosts: Les and Bess Aho

Guests frequently comment about the peace, quiet, and natural beauty of the setting. The fragrant flower and herb gardens, the birds and squirrels, can be enjoyed while sitting at the many benches placed throughout the gardens. Then stroll down the hill through the forget-me-nots to the pastoral lake. This turn-of-the-century home is a mecca of collections from advertising silhouettes to checkerboards to depression glass and Fiesta ware that the morning candlelit breakfasts feature.

Guests enjoy the many recreational facilities of the Nicolet National Forest; Camp Five and Nicolet Scenic trains; nearby casinos; Brush Run 101 World Championship Off Road Races; Barefoot Figure 8 Open, but they also have the option of just relaxing and enjoying the simple pleasures of a small town.

Irresistable Orange Date Muffins...
A Canadian Favorite

Yields: 12 large muffins

Ingredients:

1 orange
1/2 cup orange juice
1/2 cup chopped dates or raisins
1 egg
1/4 cup margarine, room temperature
1 1/2 cups all-purpose flour
1 teaspoon baking soda
1 teaspoon baking powder
3/4 cup white sugar
3/4 teaspoon salt

Procedure:

Cut orange in eighths, remove seeds, put in blender. Add orange juice and dates. Blend until liquified. Add egg and margarine, blend again.

Into large bowl sift dry ingredients. Add blender mixture to flour mixture. Stir to blend.

Fill greased muffin cups and bake at 400° for 20 minutes.

The Rhinelander Daily News wrote, "Traditional hospitality is emphasized at Courthouse Square Bed & Breakfast, and it's evident from the moment you enter this delightful home where tranquility and peace abounds. You will no doubt smell something delicious baking in Bess's kitchen, as gourmet cooking is one of her specialties."

Rates at the Courthouse Square Bed & Breakfast range from $50-$60, and include a full breakfast.

Crystal River Bed and Breakfast

E1369 Rural Road, Waupaca, WI 54981
715•258•5333

Hosts: Gene and Lois Sorensen

Waking up to the luxury of freshly brewed coffee and warm pumpkin bread on the door step of your room is just one of the treats in store for guests at the Crystal River Bed and Breakfast. Freshly ironed sheets, down comforters, locally made candy and a profusion of pillows all greet the guests as they enter. Located on the bank of the famous Crystal River just outside of Waupaca in the National Register Historic District of Rural, this unique 1853 riverside home has much to offer. Featured in *Wisconsin Trails* magazine, chosen for the inside cover of the 1990 Wisconsin Tourism publication *Winter Adventures* and being featured as the front page article of *Milwaukee Sentinel* travel section; this Bed and Breakfast offers 6 luxurious rooms, 4 with private baths, 2 with fireplaces and a private balcony overlooking the river. The Crystal River Bed and Breakfast is truly a luxurious step back in time.

Central Wisconsin is fast becoming the mecca of antique shop lovers. That, as well as the 23 spring-fed Chain-O-Lakes, Rustic Roads, Hartman Creek State Park and unique gift shops make the Waupaca area "The place to visit."

Company Eggs and Ham

serves 8

Ingredients:

8 slices of bread
2/3 cup shredded cheddar cheese (can be velveeta)
1 1/2 caps chopped ham or dried beef or crabmeat
1 4-ounce can mushrooms
1/4 cup chopped onions
8 eggs
4 cups milk
1/4 teaspoon dried mustard

Procedure:

Break up 8 slices of bread in 9" x 13" pan, greased. Add 2/3 cup shredded cheddar cheese. Add chopped ham, dried beef or crabmeat.
Beat 8 eggs and add to 4 cups of milk and 1/4 teaspoon mustard. Mix and pour over the bread, cheese, meat. Cover and let stand, 15 minutes.
Bake in 325° oven for 1 hour. Could be served with sauce such as Cream of Mushroom soup.

This can be made the night before, covered and refrigerated.

Room rates at the Crystal River Bed & Breakfast range from $50-$75. Full breakfast included.

The Cunningham House Bed and Breakfast

110 Market Street, Platteville, WI 53818
608•348•5532

Hosts: Arletta and Jud Giese

The Cunningham House was once the home of the well known surgeon Dr. Wilson Cunningham and became, in 1962, The Cunningham Museum—home of Grant Country Artifacts. In 1987 the museum moved to nearby Lancaster. Jud and Arletta then began the task of restoring the building into a home again. Now, with a new heating and air conditioning system, a new roof, gleaming floors and fresh wall paper; it is ready to welcome guests.

Guests come from all over the world to Platteville for the Shakespeare Festival, the annual Music Festival, the Chicago Bears training camp, the excellent Mining Museum, and other stellar attractions in the area.

Eggs Goldenrod

serves 2

Ingredients:

4 hard boiled eggs, shelled
2 tablespoons butter
2 tablespoons flour
1 1/4 cups milk (whole or skim)
Salt and pepper
1 raw egg yolk
2 tablespoons lemon juice
2 sliced buttered toast

Procedure:

Separate whites and yolks of hard boiled eggs. Dice whites and set aside. Reserve the yolks.

Melt the butter in a saucepan. Stir in flour, blend and cook over low heat at least 2 minutes. Slowly add milk, and cook 5 minutes, stirring constantly until sauce thickens. Add salt and pepper to taste.

In small bowl, combine the raw egg yolk and lemon juice. Stir small amount of hot sauce into lemon mixture, then add this mixture to the rest of the hot sauce. Cook until smooth and hot. Add diced egg whites.

Spoon sauce over toast. Grate egg yolks over sauce. Serve immediately with additional buttered toast.

Freshly baked muffins and fresh orange juice are part of a full breakfast offered to guests at a time of their convenience every morning.

Rates at the Cunningham House range from $45-$65, and include a full breakfast.

Dering House

251 West James, Columbus, WI 53925
414•623•2015

Hosts: Kris and Steven Sauer

Dering House is an example of unique, Prairie style architecture with craftsmanship quality. Formerly a doctor's office and home of the Columbus-Fall River party line radio program, it now offers respite to travelers.

With lots of living space—an elegant living room, upper and lower sunporches—it's a great reading getaway (books provided!). There are kitchen facilities available for extended stays, or rent the whole house for special occasions.

We are located in downtown Columbus, within easy walking distance of antique malls (including Wisconsin's largest antique mall), AMTRAK train station, downtown shops, City Hall, art gallery, library and a Sullivan "jewel-box" bank.

Be in Madison in less than 20 minutes, or, retire to the countryside and visit or stay at our one-room schoolhouse.

Swiss Turkey Quiche

6 servings

Ingredients:

1 9" unbaked pastry shell
1 cup (4 ounce) shredded Swiss cheese
2 tablespoons flour
1 tablespoon instant chicken bouillon granules
2 cups cubed, cooked turkey
1 cup milk
3 eggs, well beaten
1/4 cup chopped onion
2 tablespoons chopped green pepper
2 tablespoons chopped pimento
French fried onions

Procedure:

Preheat oven to 425°. Bake pastry shell 8 minutes; remove from oven. Reduce oven temperature to 350°.

In medium bowl, toss cheese with flour and bouillon; add remaining ingredients. Mix well. Pour into prepared shell.

Bake 40-45 minutes or until set, topping with French fried onions during last 5 minutes.

Let stand 10 minutes before serving. Refrigerate leftovers.

This recipe was shared with us by our first guests (Janet and Pete Hermanson from Story City, Iowa) and we gratefully acknowledge their contribution to our breakfast repertoire! Quiche and croissants are featured on Sundays, with other specialties during the week.

Rates at Dering House range from $40-$90, which include a full breakfast.

Dreams of Yesteryear Bed and Breakfast

1100 Brawley Street, Stevens Point, WI 54481
715•341•4525

Hosts: Bonnie and Bill Maher

The J.L. Jensen house is listed on the National Register of Historic Places. It was designed by architect J.H. Jeffers, who also designed the Wisconsin Exhibition Building for the St. Louis World's Fair (The Louisiana Purchase Exposition) in 1904. Beginning with its construction in 1901 for businessman J.L. Jensen, this house has been the focus of numerous newspaper articles. More recently, "Rejuvenating a Turn-of-the-Century Beauty," the story of its restoration by hosts Bonnie and Bill Maher, was featured in *Victorian Homes Magazine*.

Bonnie is employed at a tutoring center at the University and Bill owns a water conditioning business. Both are historical consultants and are originally from Stevens Point. They enjoy talking about their home and their community.

Morning Pumpkin Coffeecake

serves 16

Ingredients:

1 1/2 cups firmly packed brown sugar
3/4 cup (1 1/2 sticks) margarine
1 16-ounce can (1 3/4 cups) solid pack pumpkin
6 egg whites
2 tablespoons water
2 cups all-purpose flour
1 1/2 cups Quaker Oats
    (Quick or Old-Fashioned, uncooked), divided
3/4 cup raisins
1 tablespoon baking powder
2 teaspoons baking soda
2 teaspoons cinnamon

Procedure:

    Heat oven to 350°. Spray 10 inch tube or bundt pan with no stick cooking spray. Beat sugar and margarine until fluffy. Mix in pumpkin, egg whites and water. Gradually add combined flour, 1 1/4 cups oats and remaining ingredients; mix well. Spread into pan; sprinkle with remaining 1/4 cup oats.
    Bake 60-70 minutes or until wooden pick comes out clean.
    Cool 10 minutes; remove from pan.

    Note: Here's a cake that smells and tastes scrumptiously delicious and is healthy too. Relax and enjoy.

    "The Dreams" offers Victorian elegance, complete with antique furniture, lush gardens, and warm hospitality. Each morning guests are treated to a delicious gourmet breakfast, served in either the formal dining room or the sunporch overlooking the gardens. Visit Dreams of Yesteryear. It's the kind of place that "Victorian dreams are made of."

    Rates at the Dreams of Yesteryear range from $55-$75, which include a full breakfast.

East Highland Bed & Breakfast

W4342 Hwy D, Phillips, WI 54555
715•339•3492

Hosts: Jeanne and Russ Kirchmeyer

We love company, sharing our collections with visitors and Jeanne loves to cook, that's why we turned our home into a Bed & Breakfast.

It is a former school house completely done by us with lots of wood beams and floors, lace curtains, hand-hooked rugs, plants and antiques. We have three guest rooms with 2 shared baths.

A large beautifully landscaped yard with flowers and a screen house, the woods with its nature trails are yours to enjoy.

Price County is noted for its well-groomed snowmobile trails, ninety-five lakes, forty-five trout streams, and good hunting. We also have the Wisconsin Concrete Park, which is the largest collection of concrete folk art in the nation and Timm's hill, the highest point in the state.

Cherry-Cream Cheesecoffee Cake

Ingredients:

3 1/2 to 4 cups flour
1/3 cup sugar
1 teaspoon salt
  (I use 1/2 teaspoon)
1 package of yeast
1/3 cup margarine
1/2 cup water
1/2 cup milk
1 egg

FILLING:
1 8-ounce package of cream
  cheese, softened (I use lite)
1/4 cup sugar
3 tablespoons flour
1 egg yolk (save white)
1 can cherry (or apple) pie filling

TOPPING:
1/3 cup chopped pecans
1/4 cup sugar

Procedure:

In a large bowl use 2 cups of the flour and blend the sugar, salt, and yeast together.

In microwave heat the margarine, water, and milk together until margarine melts. Cool until warm and pour into flour mix. Add the egg.

With dough hooks in mixer beat for one minute. Add one more cup of flour and beat. Beat until there are no longer small brown flecks of the yeast showing.

Turn out on board and with remaining flour, knead until springy. Let raise, covered with damp towel, in warm place until double, about an hour.

Divide the dough in half, let rest a couple of minutes. Roll each piece into a 15" circle, place in two 9" round cake pans. Press into pans letting dough hang over.

Beat first 4 filling ingredients together. Spread evenly over dough. Spread cheese with half a can of cherry pie filling (or apple); repeat with other pan.

Cut dough in 1/2" strips to the filling. Bring strips to center twisting them. Brush each with beaten egg white. Divide 1/3 cup of chopped pecans and a 1/4 cup of sugar between the two; sprinkling on top. Let rise for 45 minutes. Bake in a 375° oven for 30-35 minutes.

You can cover and refrigerate for 24 hours but will take more than 45 minutes to raise them.

I bake them the same day and heat them covered in the microwave just before serving.

Rates at the East Highland Bed and Breakfast range from $45-$60, which include a full breakfast.

The Fargo Mansion Inn

406 Mulberry Street, Lake Mills, WI 53551
414•648•3654

Hosts: Barry Luce and Tom Boycks

For that memorable, romantic getaway—experience one of The Fargo Mansion Inn's elegantly appointed Victorian guest rooms. Each room features a private bath, adorned in hand-laid Italian marble. Some suites have whirlpools for two. The master suite features a whirlpool bath concealed behind a secret passageway—just ask!

After enjoying a full gourmet breakfast, a day's activities may include hiking or cross country skiing at Aztalan State Park, boating or swimming on beautiful Rock Lake, biking the Glacial Drumlin Bike Trail, or for the less adventurous, downtown historic Lake Mills provides an array of unique antique, gift and craft shops.

Listed on the National Registry of Historic Places, The Fargo Mansion Inn provides an experience you won't soon forget.

Baked Egg and Cheese Casserole

serves 6

Ingredients:

1 dozen eggs
2 cups shredded medium aged cheddar cheese
1/2 cup chopped fresh broccoli
1 small can of mushrooms, stems and pieces
1/4 cup diced green pepper
1/2 cup milk
6 tablespoons of butter

Procedure:

Preheat oven to 375°. Grease a 9" x 13" glass pan.
Sprinkle 1 cup of shredded cheese over bottom of pan. Break eggs evenly over cheese. Break yolks. Sprinkle broccoli, mushrooms, green pepper evenly over eggs. Sprinkle second cup of shredded cheese over vegetables. Drizzle milk over top. Place butter evenly over top.
Bake 30-40 minutes or until firm. Cool 5 minutes. Cut into 6 equal portions.
Garnish with parsley, sliced banana and orange.
May be prepared the night before and refrigerated.

Rates at The Fargo Mansion Inn range from $68-$145 per night, which include a full breakfast.

Ferg Haus Inn

N8599 Ferg Road, Manawa, WI 54949
414•596•2946

Hosts: Lloyd & Shirley Ferg

    The four guest rooms, with shared bath, are decorated with lace and ruffles, fluffy comforters, and hand-finished furniture. Oil paintings adorn the walls.
    Enjoy a sing-a-long around the organ in the sitting room. The setting, reminiscent of Bavaria, is a fairy-tale village. Ferg's Bavarian Village (a former farmstead) is dotted with flower boxes, elves, balconies, and shops. Located in the quiet country-side of Waupaca County.

Potato Pancakes

serves 6

Ingredients:

3 pounds uncooked potatoes
3 eggs separated
1 1/4 cups sifted flour
1/2 teaspoon salt
1 large tart apple, peeled, cored and grated
1/2 teaspoon grated onion

Procedure:

Mix egg yolks, flour, salt, grated apple and onion. Fold in stiffly beaten egg whites.
Peel potatoes, grate and add immediately to above.
Pour a small amount onto a hot griddle to make thin pancakes. Brown on both sides. Serve immediately.

Room rates at the Ferg Haus Inn are $45-$55, including a country-style breakfast.

Forgotten Tymes

7420 Tower Road, Siren, WI 54872
715•349•5837

Hosts: Al and Pat Blume

Forgotten Tymes is growing. Our Stable House is now completed, sleeps 10 with a double jacuzzi; very private! Also the 1872 School House is also completed, sleeps 8. Handicapped accessible, secluded, privacy! Or try the 1897 Honeymoon Cabin. These cabins are decorated with period furnishings, along with modern conveniences.

Hope to see you . . .

Stromboli

6 servings

Ingredients:

1 loaf frozen bread dough, thawed
1/2 pound hamburger, browned and drained
1/2 pound pork sausage, browned and drained
1/2 pound pepperoni, sliced
2 cups shredded cheese
1 egg, beaten lightly
1/2 teaspoon garlic salt or powder
1/2 teaspoon Italian seasoning
1/2 teaspoon Parsley flakes

Roll dough into 8" x 12" rectangle, about 1/4" thick. Mix egg with seasonings and brush some onto crust. Add meat and cheese. Roll and put on greased cookie sheet seam down. Brush egg mixture on top. Bake 20-30 minutes at 350°.

Serve with spaghetti sauce on side. Can also be filled with use sausage and scrambled eggs, green peppers, onions. Make your own mixture.

A very good cook by the name of Connie gave this to me.

Rates at the Forgotten Tymes range from $80-$125 or $450 a week, with a continental breakfast.

French Country Inn of Ephraim

3052 Spruce Lane, P.O. Box 129, Ephraim, WI 54211
414•854•4001

Hosts: Walt Fisher and Joan Fitzpatrick

The French Country Inn of Ephraim was built in 1912 as a summer home for a Chicago family with ten children. The house is situated on an acre of ground, a quiet garden setting with mature trees and flowers, one hundred yards from the water in the village of Ephraim in Door County.

Each of the seven summer guest rooms (four in winter) is individually decorated with period furniture and there are spacious common areas for socializing. Much of the original architecture remains, including french doors, multi-paned casement windows, and a huge stone fireplace.

The Inn is located within ten minutes of three state parks and only footsteps away from the water, so outdoor activities abound. Door County is also famous for its Fish Boils (served at many local restaurants) and artist studios (many in restored barns and log homes).

Walt's Granola

serves 14

Ingredients:

7 cups old fashioned or rolled oats
1 cup raw, unsalted, sunflower seeds
¼ teaspoon cinnamon
¼ teaspoon nutmeg
½ cup canola oil
½ cup honey

Procedure:

Mix dry ingredients together in a large bowl. Separately mix honey and oil together and add to dry ingredients. Mix thoroughly and spread on two cookie sheets.

Bake in 275° to 300° oven for 20 minutes or until golden brown. (Stir every 5 to 6 minutes to assure equal browning.) Cool completely, then store in closed container.

This is a very versatile recipe. We usually serve it in cereal bowls with fresh fruit (Door County cherries) or as granola parfaits (in a parfait glass, alternate layers of no-fat yogurt mixed with honey, fresh fruit, and granola). It is also a good topping for ice cream or frozen yogurt.

Rates at the French Country Inn range from $52-$84 May through October and $49-$59 November through April. Rates include a continental plus breakfast.

The "Gables"

821 Dodge Street, Kewaunee, WI 54216
414•388•0220

Hosts: Penny and Earl Dunbar

Relax and be Pampered! is our motto and we try hard to get you to do this. Acting as ambassadors to our area, we invite you to get the most out of your vacation time.

Stroll among 44 beautiful architectural styled homes in our Marquette Historical District. Walk along the scenic shoreline of Lake Michigan or in one of the many quiet parks. Return home refreshed.

Penny, a Registered Dietitian, can accommodate any dietary need, loves to cook, and tries new and different foods every day. We try to use Wisconsin food products in every breakfast, and coffeecakes are our specialty.

Gift certificates are available. Let us know if you are celebrating any occasion so we can make your stay extra special.

We await your phone call and would love to meet you soon . . .

Relax and be Pampered!

Criss-Cross Coffeecake

serves 6

Ingredients:

1 3-ounce package cream cheese, softened
1/4 cup butter, softened
2 cups Bisquick baking mix
2 tablespoons milk

Also needed:
Favorite homemade jam or preserves
Cinnamon sugar mixture
Frosting

Procedure:

　　Mix all ingredients together to form dough. Turn out onto floured surface and knead 10 times.
　　Roll dough into a 8" x 12" rectangle. Spread, down the center, your favorite thick fruit jam or preserves. Fold over each side of dough over filling. Cut XXX marks on top with sharp knife. Sprinkle with cinnamon sugar mixture. Place on greased cookie sheet.
　　Bake at 425° for 15 minutes. Remove from oven and place onto attractive platter. Drizzle with melted frosting.

　　Coffeecakes are our specialty and this one is very versatile. We use any seasonal fruit made into jam.

Rates at the "Gables" range from $50-$65, which include a full breakfast.

The Gray Goose Bed and Breakfast

4258 Bay Shore Drive, Sturgeon Bay WI 54235
414•743•9100

Hosts: Jack and Jessie Burkhardt

Located well out of the city on a quiet, wooded site next to an apple orchard, The Gray Goose epitomizes the term "country," which is really what Door County always was, and what most visitors want it to remain.

This is one of the very few Bed & Breakfasts in the "Cape Cod of the Midwest" with a real view of woods and water. In the true tradition of bed-and-breakfast inns you'll find warm, personal hospitality; a full, delicious, "skip-lunch" breakfast; seasonal snacks and beverages; plenty of space to just kick back and take it easy; shared baths; and hosts ready to help you in every way.

This is an 1862 home with the entire second floor made over especially for guests and furnished with authentic antiques. There are many windows for air, light, and just looking; four large rooms with luxurious bedding; a guest sitting room with games, piano, and cable TV; a full front porch with old wicker and a swing; and a strikingly beautiful dining room where guests breakfast together by candle, lamp, and sunlight at an 1874 table whose setting changes every day.

Swedish Pears

serves 4-6

Ingredients:

4 large pears
1 lemon
6 tablespoons butter (or margarine)
8 tablespoons sugar
1 1/2 tablespoons flour
2 tablespoons cream (or half-and-half)
1/2 cup slivered almonds.

Procedure:

Peel, slice, and core pears. Cut lemon and squeeze over pears as they are sliced to prevent browning. Put pears in buttered glass pie pan. Melt butter. Add sugar and flour. Heat until thick and smooth (4-5 minutes). Stir in cream and almonds. Pour mixture over pears. Bake at 350° for 30 minutes or until pears are soft. Top each serving with nutmeg.

This special dish, only one of many served at The Gray Goose where breakfast courses vary each day, can also be made with apples, such as Granny Smiths. Ingredient amounts can be increased to serve more guests. And it can be made the night before, refrigerated, and baked in the morning. It's a delightfully different way to serve pears, a fruit treat guests really enjoy.

Rates at The Gray Goose range from $65-$75 per night and include a full gourmet breakfast plus seasonal snacks and beverages.

Greystone Farm's Bed and Breakfast

N9391 Adams Road, East Troy, WI 53120
414•495•8485

Hosts: Fred and Ruth Leibner

Greystone Farm has been our home for over thirty years; the place where we raised our six children and the "gathering spot" for both their friends and ours.

The kitchen is truly the heart of this home. If the walls could speak, they would whisper of children's laughter, of evenings spent, of the meaning of family. This is the favorite room where memories were made. The wonderful smells coming from the kitchen bring back remembrances of growing up.

On our farm, springtime brought with it fresh asparagus, strawberries and rhubarb along with the scents of apple, pear and plum blossoms reminding us of the harvest yet to come.

This recipe has always been a favorite of ours—we hope it will awaken a memory in you.

Springtime Rhubarb Pie ... Wisconsin Style

serves 6-8

Ingredients:

4 tablespoons butter
3 cups diced fresh rhubarb
1 1/2 cups sugar
6 tablespoons cream or half and half
6 tablespoons additional sugar
1/2 teaspoon salt
4 tablespoons cornstarch
3 egg yolks, well beaten
1 baked 9" pie shell

Procedure:

Melt butter in saucepan. Add 1 1/2 cups sugar and the fresh rhubarb. Cook until tender.

Combine rest of ingredients and add them to the rhubarb. Cook and stir until thick. Pour into baked pie shell. Chill thoroughly. You can top it with meringue but we prefer it plain.

Rates at the Greystone Farm's Bed and Breakfast range from $45-$80 per night, which include a full breakfast.

Harrisburg Inn Bed and Breakfast

W3334 Hwy 35, P.O. Box 15, Maiden Rock, WI 54750
715•448•4500

Hosts: Carol Crisp and Bern Paddock

Imagine yourself seated on the front porch of the Harrisburg Inn, fragrant steaming coffee and the aromas of fruity muffins and cheesey eggs filling your senses. Then let your gaze wander over twenty-some miles of sparkling water and curving bluffs as the wide Mississippi spreads before you. That's what brings guests to our little village and inn overlooking Lake Pepin of the Mississippi. No matter what the season, breakfast is always served with the view. Private baths and queen beds in each of the sunny bedrooms enhance your comfort. Come let us wrap you in the warm embrace of our old house by the river and Inn-joy!

Carol's Harrisburg Breakfast Casserole

serves 6-8

Ingredients:

1/2 to 3/4 cup finely diced ham
1/2 cup sliced green onions or chopped white onion
1/2 to 3/4 cup chopped fresh mushrooms or 8 ounces canned
Optional:
1/2 cup shredded carrot
1/2 cup chopped broccoli

FILLING:
2 cups shredded Swiss and/or cheddar cheese
5 large eggs
2 heaping tablespoons dijon mustard (Grey Poupon)
1 teaspoon Original Mrs. Dash seasoning
1/4 teaspoon black pepper
1 teaspoon parsley flakes
1 teaspoon chives (optional)
1/2 cup Bisquick
Milk to make 3 cups of batter

Procedure:

You can be as generous with filling as desired!
Grease or spray with non-stick cooking spray 6 individual casseroles or ramekins or a deep 9" glass pie plate. Layer in onion, mushrooms, and diced ham. For vegetarian style, omit ham and add shredded carrot, chopped broccoli. Top with shredded Swiss cheese and/or cheddar.
Beat eggs in measuring pitcher. Add seasoning and Bisquick. Blend. Add milk to make 3 cups batter. Pour 1/2 cup batter over each casserole. Bake at 400°F until puffed and golden, about 30 minutes. We often pass salsa and corn muffins with our casseroles.

Rates at the Harrisburg Inn range from $55-$88 plus tax, which include a full breakfast.

Hill Street Bed and Breakfast

353 Hill Street, Spring Green, WI 53588
608•588•7751

Hostess: Doris Randall

In the early 1900's, this Queen Anne style house was the show place of Spring Green. Although Jim and Marie Neider preserved much of the house's original charm in their restoration, it is not just the hand carved woodwork that makes it home away from home.

Add your life to the lives of the people for whom the six guest rooms have been named. Form new friendships in this family atmosphere. Gather with others around the piano for music and laughter. Ask your hostess about the legend and lore of Spring Green, or places to explore today. Join the Hill Street family and look forward to next year's reunion.

Oven Puffed French Toast

serves 6-8

Ingredients:

French bread, cut 1 1/2" thick, 8 slices
6 eggs
1/8 teaspoon nutmeg
1/4 teaspoon cinnamon
1/4 teaspoon mace
1 teaspoon vanilla
3 cups half and half

Topping:

1/2 cup firm butter, cubed
2 tablespoons dark corn syrup
1 cup brown sugar
1 cup nuts

Procedure:

    Place bread slices in a single layer in a generously buttered 9" x 13" x 2" baking pan. Combine eggs, spices, vanilla and half-and-half, mixing well.
    Pour over bread slices, cover and refrigerate overnight. Before baking, baste unabsorbed liquid over bread. Combine topping ingredients until the mixture resembles a coarse texture. Sprinkle over bread slices and bake in preheated oven at 350° for 40 minutes. Serve hot.

Room rates at Hill Street range from $50-$75, which include a full breakfast.

Hillcrest Inn and Carriage House

540 Storle Avenue, Burlington, WI 53105
414•763•4706

Hosts: Dick and Karen Granholm

Picture yourself on a spacious porch watching a lovely sunset, strolling through flower gardens, or just relaxing at this serene four-acre estate. Built in 1908 Hillcrest boasts the most magnificent view in southeastern Wisconsin.

Dick and Karen Granholm are experienced bed and breakfast travellers who offer guests the amenities and luxuries they desire . . . private baths, queen-size beds, full breakfasts, fireplaces, double whirlpools, air-conditioning, and a smoke-free environment.

The six rooms are beautifully decorated and furnished with period antiques. Experience this majestic Inn and Carriage House located in Burlington, Chocolate City, USA.

Oatmeal Pancakes

about 16 pancakes

Ingredients:

1/2 cup flour
1 cup uncooked oatmeal
2 cups buttermilk
1 tablespoon sugar
1 tablespoon cornmeal
1 teaspoon soda
1/4 teaspoon salt
3 tablespoons melted butter
4 eggs, separated

Procedure:

Mix oatmeal and buttermilk and soak overnight. Mix all other ingredients (except egg whites) together thoroughly. Add to oatmeal and buttermilk mixture. Beat egg whites stiff and fold into other ingredients just before cooking. Fry on hot, oiled griddle until golden brown.
Serve with butter, maple syrup or jam.

Rates at the Hillcrest Inn range from $60-$150, which include a full breakfast.

Historic Bennett House

825 Oak Street, Wisconsin Dells, WI 53965
608•254•2500

Hosts: Rich and Gail Obermeyer

Relax in this quiet stately 1863 home listed on the National Historic Register and featured in Midwest Living Magazine.

Located one block from downtown Dells, it enables walking to scenic Wisconsin River, Antique Mall, toy and doll museum, famous boat and duck tours down the river, Dells attractions, and food.

European style decor and world famous Bennett photographs and stereos adorn the home.

Enjoy 130 years of heritage with us.

Peach French Toast Supreme

serves 6-8

Ingredients:

SAUCE:
1 — 29 ounce can peach slices, drained
1 small can apricot nectar
1/4 cup white sugar
1/4 teaspoon almond extract
1/2 teaspoon cinnamon
1 tablespoon brandy (optional)
3 tablespoons cornstarch

FRENCH TOAST:
5 eggs
1 1/2 cups milk
1 teaspoon vanilla
1 stick (1/2 cup) butter
1 cup dark brown sugar
2 tablespoons water
12 slices of French bread

Procedure:

SAUCE:
   Mix cornstarch with sugar and cinnamon. Whisk into juices, almond extract, and brandy. Heat and stir until thickened. Serve over hot French toast.

FRENCH TOAST:
   Mix together the eggs, milk, and vanilla in a bowl. Set aside
   In a sauce pan mix the butter, brown sugar and water. Heat until mixture bubbles, stir (mixture looks foamy). Pour into 9" x 13" pan. Place drained peaches on top of brown sugar mixture. Cover fruit with slices of bread. Pour milk mixture over. Cover and refrigerate overnight.
   Next day, uncover, and bake 350° for 40 minutes.
   For each serving: Pour hot sauce over and top with dollop of sour cream. Serve with your favorite breakfast sausage.

Rates at the Historic Bennett House range from $65 to $85 per night and include a luscious fireside breakfast.

The Inn

104 Wisconsin Avenue, Montreal, WI 54550
715•561•5180

Hosts: Dick and Doris Schumacher

The Inn is part of the town of Montreal which was formerly owned by an iron mining company. The city of Montreal is listed on the National Register of Historic Places.

The Inn is furnished with comfortable family antiques and quilts. Photos and memorabilia of the building's mining past decorate the rooms. The building served as the offices of the mining company from 1913 until 1962 when the mines closed. The original vault system in the building now houses a sauna for guests. Guests can ski the cross country trails through the pine forests, around the mine tailings, from the front door of The Inn or downhill ski at one of the five major area ski hills. It is a short drive to Lake Superior, 50 water falls, and Copper Falls State Park.

Pecan Twist Rolls

makes 16 rolls

Ingredients:

2 cups all purpose flour
2 tablespoons sugar
1 tablespoon baking soda
1/2 teaspoon salt
1/4 cup butter
1/4 cup margarine
1 egg
1/2 cup milk
3 tablespoons brown sugar
1/4 cup VERY finely chopped pecans

Procedure:

Sift together flour, sugar, baking powder, and salt. Cut in butter and margarine. Mixture will resemble coarse crumbs. Add beaten egg and milk.
Stir only until dough clings together (like a pie crust).
Knead gently on floured board. Roll dough to 16" x 8" rectangle. Brush with butter. Combine pecans and brown sugar. Sprinkle on top and pat into dough. Fold dough lengthwise and pat together. Cut into 16 one-inch strips. Hold by ends and gently twist twice in opposite direction. Place on lightly greased baking sheet. Press ends of twists down.
Bake at 450° for 10 minutes.

Rates at The Inn range from $40-$70, which include a full breakfast.

Inn at Grady's Farm

W10928 Hwy 33, Portage, WI 53901
608•742•3627

Hostesses: Carol Mueller and Donna Obright

The Inn is a 14-room Victorian farmhouse, furnished with antiques throughout, including our 4 spacious bedrooms with private baths. Also for our guests' use we have a large library, including a video tape library, jacuzzi-spa room done in a jungle motif and complimentary refreshments.

Abundant farm breakfast is served at individual tables in our sunny dining room, or on our screened-in veranda.

Three miles of the Baraboo River meander through the 300 acres accessible to our guests. Canoe rentals, including overnight trips are available.

We are located right off of I-90/94 on Hwy 33, across from Cascade Mountain, near Devils Head, and close to all the Dells/Baraboo attractions.

Rarebit Au Gratin

serves 6

Ingredients:

2 tablespoons butter or margarine
1 cup soft breadcrumbs
1/4 cup grated Parmesan cheese
1 tablespoon snipped chives
1 teaspoon paprika
Rarebit Sauce, see below
18 slices bacon
6 thick tomato slices
6 English muffins, split, toasted, buttered

RAREBIT SAUCE:
2 egg yolks
1 cup shredded American cheese (4 ounces)
1 cup shredded Swiss (4 ounces)
1 1/4 cups half and half
1 teaspoon dry mustard
2 teaspoons Worcestershire

Procedure:

Preheat oven to 350°. In a small saucepan, melt butter. Add breadcrumbs, Parmesan cheese, chives and paprika; toss and set aside. In large skillet, cook bacon over medium heat until crisp. Drain on paper towels. Reserve 3 tablespoons drippings in skillet. Cook tomato slices in drippings until tender. Place 6 of the muffin halves in 6 individual au gratin dishes. Cut remaining muffin halves crosswise, and place 2 pieces cutside down along edges of each dish. Place a tomato slice and 3 slices of bacon on top of each muffin half. Place au gratin dishes in oven while preparing Rarebit Sauce. Ladle sauce over muffin stacks in au gratin dishes. Top with the breadcrumb mixture.
Bake 15-20 minutes or until bubbly and browned.
To prepare sauce, in a bowl, beat egg yolks and set aside. In heavy saucepan, mix American, Swiss cheese, half-and-half, dry mustard and Worcestershire sauce. Stir constantly over low heat until melted. Take one cup of this hot cheese sauce and mix into egg yolks. Then take this egg yolk mixture and add back into the rest of the hot cheese in saucepan. Stir constantly over medium heat until mixture thickens.
For Variety: Substitute grilled tomato and bacon with steamed broccoli spears rolled up in ham slice.

Rates at the Inn at Grady's Farm range from $45-$55 per night, which include a full breakfast.

The Inn at Pinewood

P.O. Box 549, 1800 Silver Forest Lane, Eagle River, WI 54521
715•479•4114

Hosts: Edward and Nona Soroosh

Warmest hospitality awaits you the minute you arrive at the Inn at Pinewood. This delightful Northwoods Bed and Breakfast Inn, offers you a truly unique experience.

The comfortable guest rooms all have private baths, king size beds and balconies overlooking the lake or woods. Some of the rooms have double whirlpool baths and fireplaces.

This twenty-one room Inn, located on the shore of Carpenter Lake, consists of eight guest rooms, a parlor with a huge stone fireplace, libraries, great room, garden dining room, recreation room, etc.

Wake up to the aroma of freshly baked muffins and breads and enjoy a leisurely breakfast. A favorite of the Inn's guests are Cranberry Nut Muffins. Since Eagle River is a major cranberry growing area, berries are bought in the fall and frozen for use all year.

After breakfast, spend your days boating, hiking, golfing, playing tennis, or browsing through the unique shops in the area. In the winter, cross-country ski, just two miles away in the Nicolet National Forest, or snowmobile, then return to the Inn and relax by the fire.

Enjoy a romantic retreat anytime of the year.

Spiced Cranberry Nut Muffins

18 muffins

Ingredients:

2 cups flour
1 cup sugar
1 1/2 teaspoons baking powder
1/2 teaspoon baking soda
1 1/2 teaspoons nutmeg
1 teaspoon cinnamon
1/2 teaspoon ginger
1/2 cup shortening
3/4 cup orange juice
1 teaspoon vanilla
2 eggs slightly beaten
2 teaspoons orange rind
1 1/2 cups cranberries
1 1/2 cup chopped pecans

Procedure:

In a large bowl, mix flour, sugar, baking powder, baking soda, nutmeg, cinnamon and ginger.

With a pastry blender, cut in shortening. Add orange juice, vanilla, eggs, and orange rind. Add cranberries and nuts. Mix only to blend.

Spoon into 18 greased muffin tins. Bake in a 350° oven for 25 minutes, or until golden brown.

Rates at The Inn at Pinewood range from $65-$105 per night, which include a full breakfast.

Jefferson-Day House

1109 3rd Street, Hudson, WI 54016
715•386•7111

Hosts: Sharon and Wally Miller

After a romantic evening in a whirlpool for two gazing at a fireplace, guests enjoy memorable four-course breakfasts. These breakfasts are served either fireside in the dining room, in a sunroom in one of the suites, or on the back patio. Guests learn about some of the Miller's collections of depression glass, Maxfield Parrish prints, Roseville pottery, and Fiesta-ware. Also, Wally, a former choir director, plays his guitar and sings the dessert song at the end of the meal.

Danebod Pancakes

serves 6-8

Ingredients:

3 cups flour
3 teaspoons salt
2 tablespoons sugar
1 1/2 teaspoons baking soda
2 teaspoons baking powder
5 eggs
1/2 cup oil
1 quart buttermilk

Procedure:

Mix all together and cook on hot griddle. (380° for electric frypan.)

These pancakes are special because they are so light and tasty. Serve with syrup or special sauce such as fresh raspberries (blended) mixed with soft butter.

Rates at the Jefferson-Day House range from $89-$159 per night, which include a full breakfast on weekends, and a continental breakfast weekdays.

Jeremiah Mabie Bed and Breakfast

A Home Away From Home

711 E. Walworth Avenue, Delavan, WI 53115
414•728•1876

Hostess: Alberta (Bertie) Schoen

Each room is uniquely decorated and air conditioned. The inn has a mini library and a large wrap around porch for your sitting pleasure. Full breakfast from 8:30 a.m. to 9:00 a.m., served in a formal dining room. Open year round.

Jeremiah Mabie Bed and Breakfast was built in 1865 by a circus entrepreneur. He came to Delavan in 1847, with his circus from New York, initiating the circus era in the midwest and was followed by 92 circuses including Barnum & Baily.

Come and relax. Enjoy romantic guest rooms and the whirlpool in affordable elegance.

Golf—horses—dog track—boat rides, etc.

No smoking. No pets.

Bertie's Pineapple Breakfast Rolls

yield 6 servings

Ingredients:

1/2 cup packed brown sugar
1/2 cup soft butter
3/4 cup drained crushed pineapple
1 teaspoon cinnamon
1 can refrigerated biscuits

Procedure:

Melt brown sugar and butter in 8 or 9-inch square cake pan. Add pineapple and cinnamon; mix well. Place biscuits on top. Bake at 425° for 10 minutes or until done.

Rates at the Jeremiah Mabie range from $55-$95, which include a full breakfast.

Johnson Inn

231 W. North Street, P.O. Box 487, Plainfield, WI 54966
715•335•4383

Proprietors: Roger and Lois Johnson
Hosts: Burrell and Nancy Johnson

Johnson Inn welcomes you with 1800's elegance including white pillars, carved oak paneling and beautiful birch floors. Two open stairways, two fireplaces, and Amish quilts on all beds are special features. The four guest rooms are newly renovated and have Victorian decor. An excellent full breakfast is served. Hospitality is our specialty.

Johnson Inn is nestled in a quiet, small town atmosphere minutes from larger cities. Antiquing, cross-country and downhill skiing, hunting and much more are nearby. Bikes are available for guest use. Tennis courts and miniature golf are next door.

Leave all of your day-to-day worries on the doorstep at The Johnson Inn. We hope to see you soon.

Pecan Horns

36 to 48 horns

Ingredients:

1 cup COLD butter, cut up
1—8 ounce package cream cheese, cut up
2 cups all purpose flour
2/3 cups sugar
1 tablespoon ground cinnamon
1 1/4 cups finely chopped pecans
1/4 cup melted butter

POWDERED SUGAR GLAZE:
   (Makes 1/3 cup)
1 cup powdered sugar
1/2 teaspoon vanilla
1-2 tablespoons milk

Procedure:

In mixing bowl cut 1 cup butter and cream cheese into flour until pieces are the size of coarse crumbs. Divide and press mixture into 3 balls. In a small bowl, stir together sugar and cinnamon; set aside. On a lightly floured surface, slightly flatten 1 ball. Then roll dough into a 13" circle, brush with some of the melted butter, cinnamon mixture and pecans. Cut circle into 12-16 wedges (12 will give you a larger crescent, while 16 will give a daintier crescent). Roll up wedges, starting at the wide end and rolling toward points. Place pastries, point side down on ungreased cookie sheet. Repeat with remaining dough. Bake in 350° oven for 18-20 minutes or until bottoms are golden. Cool on wire racks, drizzle glaze over tops, or if rushed for time dust with powdered sugar.

GLAZE:
   Make a glaze of drizzling consistency.

NOTE INNKEEPERS:
   Prepare and shape as directed above, but do not bake. Place horns in a single layer on baking sheet and freeze. Place in freezer bags for storage in freezer. To serve, place FROZEN horns on baking sheets, bake as directed. Open the kitchen door and let the aroma awaken your guest.

Rates at the Johnson Inn range from $40-$75, which include a full breakfast.

Journey's End

203 Laconia, P.O. Box 185, Amherst, WI 54406
715•824•3970

Hosts: Jim and Genny Jewell

Nestled in the heart of scenic Wisconsin, the Journey's End Bed and Breakfast is close to many attractions for adventure-seeking sightseers and outdoor sports enthusiasts.

Whether you're staying the night or the weekend, the Journey's End Bed and Breakfast is a relaxing and warm experience you won't forget. Enjoy Jim and Genny's country style hospitality and delicious home-cooked breakfasts.

Open year round, this turn of the century Victorian mansion features large, comfortable bedrooms with some shared baths. Relax in today's comfort, surrounded by yesterday's charm. We are proud to announce this home was accepted to the National Register of Historic Homes in 1992.

Make your journey's end our Journey's End Bed and Breakfast.

Oatmeal Raspberry Bar Cookies

makes 24 - 2" x 1 1/2" bars

Ingredients:

1/2 cup room temperature butter
1/2 cup light brown sugar
1 cup flour
1/4 teaspoon baking soda
1/8 teaspoon salt
1 cup rolled oats
3/4 cup raspberry jam (seedless)

Procedure:

Heat oven to 350°. Butter or vegetable spray on 8" square pan, line with aluminum foil and butter or spray the foil. Mix all the ingredients together except the jam. Press 2 cups of the mixture into bottom of pan. Spread the jam to within 1/4" of the edge. Sprinkle the remaining crumb mixture over the top and lightly press it into the jam. Bake 35 to 40 minutes and allow to cool on a wire rack before cutting.

Rates at Journey's End range from $40-$60 per night, which include a hearty country breakfast.

Just-N-Trails Bed and Breakfast

Route 1, Box 274, Sparta, WI 54656
608•269•4522

Hosts: Don and Donna Justin

Just-N-Trails is a third generation working dairy farm that features five rooms in a 1920 Neo-Nothing farmhouse decorated with Laura Ashley linens and country decor. Several separate new or renovated country cottages provide privacy, tranquility and freedom. Warm yourself, enjoy a picnic or good conversation in the lodge complete with indoor bathrooms and snack shop in winter.

Just-N-Trails specializes in recreation—cross-country ski out the back door onto 20K of groomed and tracked trails; hike or mountain bike, pet the calves, participate in a night hike or summer hay ride.

Ride the Elroy-Sparta Bike Trail, canoe the scenic rivers, visit Amish handcraft shops, view world class scenery along the Mississippi River.

Just-N-Trails is located in a private valley surrounded by hills so relaxation is easy. The double whirlpools, fireplaces and country cottages are perfect for a romantic get-away.

Just-N-Trails Sinful Muffins

Makes 2 dozen muffins

Ingredients:

3 cups flour
3 teaspoons baking powder
3/4 teaspoon salt
1 cup sugar
1 teaspoon baking soda
2/3 cup oil or butter
1 cup YoJ Orange (yogurt juice)
2/3 cup chocolate chips
1 — 11 ounce can mandarin oranges, drained
2 eggs

TOPPING:
1 cup shredded coconut
2 tablespoons melted butter
1/3 cup sugar

Procedure:

    Mix flour, baking powder, salt, sugar, soda, oil, yogurt juice, chocolate chips, mandarin oranges, and eggs in large mixing bowl. Mix just until blended.
    Use ice cream scoop to scoop batter into paper lined muffin tins. Mix topping ingredients and sprinkle on top of muffins.
    Bake 20 minutes at 350° until golden brown.

Rates at the Just-N-Trails range from $60-$195, which include a full breakfast.

Knollwood House Bed and Breakfast

Bed and Breakfast

N8257 950th St.-Knollwood Drive, River Falls, WI 54022
715•425•1040; 800•435•0628

Hosts: Jim and Judy Tostrud

Guests can go hiking or skiing on 80 acres of beautiful Wisconsin countryside, drive golf balls from 3 tees, relax in the hot tub or go for a refreshing swim in the outdoor pool before eating a wonderful breakfast served in the solarium.

Country Breakfast Casserole is one of our guests' favorite dishes and is usually served with hot blueberry muffins.

We delight in having guests enjoy the 1886 Brick farmhouse decorated with many family heirlooms. Located 15 minutes from the Great River Road and 45 minutes from the Mall of America, guests visit from all over the world.

Old fashioned country charm with a touch of today.

Country Breakfast Casserole

serves 8-10

Ingredients:

2—12 ounce packages frozen "hot" sausage
1—2 pound package frozen hashbrowns
2—8 ounce packages shredded colby jack cheese (4 cups divided)
1 medium onion minced (1 cup)
2 cups milk
1/2 teaspoon salt
6 eggs slightly beaten
1-12 ounce carton salsa

Procedure:

    Brown and drain sausage. Combine all other ingredients except salsa and 1 cup of the cheese. Pour into 9" x 13" greased baking dish. Top with remaining cheese. Can be refrigerated overnight.
    Bake uncovered in 350° oven until knife comes out clean—50-55 minutes. Let stand 10 minutes—covered. Cut into squares. Serve with salsa in a separate dish.

    Our guests LOVE this dish. They always ask for the recipe which, by the way, was sent to us by a guest.
    We usually serve fresh blueberry muffins with this dish.

Rates at the Knollwood House range from $60-$100 which include a full breakfast.

The Kraemer House Bed and Breakfast

1190 Spruce Street, Plain, WI 53577
608•546•3161

Hosts: Gwen and Duane Kraemer

Our two-story colonial home, est. 1965 is well kept and maintained; it is complemented by a meticulous lawn and flower garden. The guest rooms are light and airy, have been redecorated and furnished with a few lovingly restored family antiques.

Wake-up coffee is provided and a full homemade breakfast varies from day to day.

The Kraemer House became a Bed and Breakfast when the local Spring Green motels could no longer accommodate the demand for lodging, due to tourist interest and popularity of the House on the Rock and American Players Theatre.

The village of Plain offers a quiet, relaxed retreat from busy city life. A nine-hole golf course, outdoor swimming pool, hard surface tennis courts and pleasant walks with jogging trails in all directions. A bikers paradise with country roads awaiting.

Just 7 miles away is Spring Green and the home of Frank Lloyd Wright's beloved "Tailisen."

Elegant Egg Puff

serves 2-4

Ingredients:

2/3 cup chopped ham (turkey ham is very good)
2/3 cup grated yellow or white cheese
2 teaspoons Dijon mustard (heaping)
3 teaspoons lite salad dressing (Hellmans)
1 teaspoon horseradish (more if you like)
2 teaspoons onion (finely chopped)
4 slices white or wheat bread (I trim the crust)
Tabasco sauce (a couple shakes)
Paprika
2 eggs
1 1/3 cups milk

Procedure:

    Grease four ovenproof dishes (ramakins). In a medium bowl, combine the ham, cheese, mustard, salad dressing, horseradish, and onions plus a few shakes of Tabasco sauce. Makes two sandwiches. Cut each diagonally into four pieces. Place two pieces of sandwich in each of the prepared dishes, arranging so the points are on top.
    In a small bowl combine the eggs and milk. Whisk well. Pour over the sandwich pieces. Sprinkle with paprika. Refrigerate overnite. Bake in a 325-350° oven for 30 to 35 minutes. This recipe can be doubled very easily.

    I like to take out of the ramakin dish and place on serving plate and garnish with a couple of slices of tomatoes and parsley.

Rates at the Kraemer House range from $50-$75, which include a full breakfast.

The Krupp Farm Homestead

W1982 Kiel Road, Route 2, New Holstein, WI 53061
414•782•5421 (reservations), 414•894•3195 (farm)

Hosts: Marion Krupp Marsh and family

The Krupp Farm Homestead is a five generation, family owned, country bed and breakfast home situated in the picturesque, rolling hills of the St. Anne area. A 360-acre dairy farm surrounds the refurbished farm house, some sections of the house date back to 1858. The living room, with a beamed ceiling of hand hewn logs rescued from the old barn, has a cozy fireplace for guests to enjoy. The farm breakfast is served in the dining room which has an original turn-of-the-century tin ceiling. Meanwhile, upstairs, guests will find five comfortable guest rooms each decorated with family heirlooms and antiques.

The Farm Homestead is ideally located—within 10 miles of Road America at Elkhart Lake, close to the historic Old Wade House at Greenbush, and near the hiking and cross-country ski trails at the Northern Kettle Moraine State Forest. Guests often stay here while attending the Experimental Aviation Association Fly-In held each August in nearby Oshkosh. Schwarz's Supper Club, a regional favorite, is found in St. Anne.

Dairyman, Dan Krupp, gives first class tours of the dairy operation. Guests are also free to roam the farmland and woods.

6-Week Bran Muffins

4 dozen muffins (depending on size)

Ingredients:

1 quart buttermilk
1 — 12 ounce box raisin bran cereal
5 eggs
1 cup vegetable oil
1 1/2 cups sugar
5 cups flour
1 tablespoon baking soda
1/2 teaspoon cinnamon
1 teaspoon vanilla
1 cup coarsely chopped nuts
2 cups raisins

Procedure:

In a large bowl mix the buttermilk and cereal. Set aside.
In another large bowl, beat the eggs. Add the vegetable oil and sugar. Mix. Add to the bran mixture in the first bowl.
Now add in flour, baking soda, cinnamon, vanilla, chopped nuts and raisins. Mix well.
Store in covered airtight container in refrigerator. Keeps up to 6 weeks. Bake as many as needed in paper muffin cups 350° for 20 minutes. Serve warm with farm butter and homemade jam!

Guests enjoy these muffins—they're always moist and fresh.
I've never kept this mixture for 6 weeks—they're always gone quickly!

Rates at the Krupp's range from $45-$70, which include a full farm breakfast.

Lambs Inn Bed and Breakfast

Route 2, Box 144, Richland Center, WI 53581
608•585•4301

Hosts: Dick and Donna Messerschmidt

Looking for peace and tranquility? Visit our 180-acre dairy farm located in the hidden valley of Little Willow, three miles out of Richland Center. Relax on the porch of our 1800's completely renovated farmhouse or on the deck of our new little cottage where you can watch deer and other wildlife as well as the dairy farm activities. Other favorite activities are feeding the trout in the spring, enjoying the spectacular scenery, antiquing or biking the backroads where you may occasionally meet an Amish buggy. Located nearby is Spring Green and Wisconsin Dells.

A special event in early to mid-May is the morel mushroom festival in Muscoda. Our guests enjoy searching for the delicate morels in our woods. In the fall the hills display breathtaking color and the local apple orchards have open houses with demonstrations and fresh cider.

Our Bed and Breakfast's four guest rooms have private baths and are furnished with country antiques. Coffee, tea and seasonal drinks are always available with fresh baked "yummies" and nightly popcorn is a family tradition.

Camp of the Woods Bread Pudding

serves 12

Ingredients:

1/2 gallon milk, scalded
1 1/2 cups sugar
1 1/2 teaspoons salt
2 tablespoons cornstarch
9 eggs
1/8 cup vanilla
1/2 cup raisins, softened in hot water and drained
8 slices bread (approximately 3 cups), trim crusts and cube

Procedure:

Mix sugar, salt and cornstarch. Add eggs, mix gently and add milk and vanilla. Place bread in bottom of buttered 9" x 13" pan. Sprinkle with raisins. Cover with milk mixture. Sprinkle with nutmeg and cinnamon.

Place 9" x 13" pan on a jelly roll pan. Fill remaining space in jelly roll pan with water, until 3/4 full.

Bake at 350° for approximately 45 minutes until knife inserted in center comes out clean. Serve warm with whipped cream or cool whip.

We acquired this recipe from the chef at the conference center in the Adirondack Mountains which served gourmet food. We spent the summer working there before we bought the family farm to renovate as a Bed and Breakfast. This is a favorite of our guests; it is just like Gramma used to make.

Room rates at the Lambs Inn are $70 for 2 people. Cottage rates are $125 for 4 people. All include a full breakfast.

Lumberman's Mansion Inn

P.O. Box 885, Hayward, WI 54843
715•634•3012

Hosts: Jan Hinrichs Blaedel and Wendy Hinrichs Sanders

Breakfast at the Lumberman's Mansion Inn is the essence of Gemutlichkeit, reflective of our German culture. Friendly conversation and smiles complement the breakfasts we prepare which always include a fresh, home-baked Kaffee Kuchen or other pastry.

The smells emanating from our kitchen at the Inn are reminiscent of those found in our home when we were children. Our mother taught us both to cook, often using recipes from her mother and grandmother. Our mom remembers enjoying these doughnuts frequently during the early part of this century when she visited her Grandma Flamm—Big Grandma—as our mom describes tall and robust.

We take great pride in the history of our Inn, the richness of our German traditions, the uniqueness of our regional flavors and the wealth of our family heritage. We get special pleasure in sharing these treasures with our guests.

Great Grandma's Drop Doughnuts

makes 2 dozen

Ingredients:

1 egg slightly beaten
1/2 cup sugar
2 tablespoons oil
1/2 cup milk
2 1/2 cups flour
2 teaspoons (heaping) baking powder
1 teaspoon nutmeg

Procedure:

Beat egg; add sugar, oil, milk. Sift together flour, baking powder and nutmeg; add to mixture 1/3 at a time, stirring after each addition. Dough will be stiff. Refrigerate while heating oil. (May be refrigerated for several days.)

Drop into hot oil (we use a fry-baby) by teaspoonful. Turn once. Fry until brown. Drain.

Shake in bag of powdered sugar to coat. (You can also use a mixture of cinnamon/sugar or just granulated sugar.) Eat hot!

Rates at the Lumberman's Mansion range from $55-$100, which include a full breakfast.

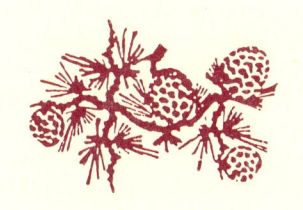

Martha's Ethnic Bed and Breakfast

226 2nd Street, Westfield, WI 53964
608•296•3361

Hosts: Ronald and Martha Polacek

Martha's Ethnic Bed and Breakfast is conveniently located between Madison and Stevens Point in Westfield—one block off of Highway 51. Here guests find a cozy turn-of-the-century American Four-Square home with three distinctive "ethnic" bedrooms of English, German and Czechoslovakian decor.

Martha's is a great place to enjoy life's simple pleasures: biking, birdwatching, star gazing, hunting, fishing, reading, walking, antiquing, good conversation, or relaxing on the front porch with morning coffee or afternoon refreshments.

A choice of three full, hearty "ethnic" breakfasts are served—each can easily take you through the day. We also offer escorted scenic drives or a trip to our favorite lake for swimming. We are happy to accommodate your special needs including meeting you at the airport in Madison.

German Farm Breakfast

serves 6

Ingredients:

6 medium potatoes boiled the night before and chilled
1/4 cup chopped onion
1 cup cut up ham, small cubes
1/4 cup water
6-8 eggs
Salt
Pepper
1 tablespoon soy sauce or other seasoning
2 tablespoons oil or margarine

Procedure:

Slice potatoes into hot oil or margarine, add onion and ham. Saute at 300° (an electric fry pan works well). Beat eggs, water and seasonings in a separate bowl. Pour over potato mixture and cook slowly at 300° until eggs are well done. Serve with whole grain bread and apple butter for an excellent breakfast that lasts all day.

Rates at Martha's Ethnic Bed and Breakfast range from $35-$65, which include a full breakfast.

The Middleton Beach Inn

2303 Middleton Beach Road, Middleton, WI 53562
608•831•6446

Owners: Tom and Shirley Duesler
Hosts: Brad and Diane Duesler

    The sunshine sparkling on the early morning waters of Lake Mendota is just one of the things that makes breakfast special at the Middleton Beach Inn. Our Raspberry Stuffed French Toast is one of the other special treats.
    You're invited to come explore the unique accommodations, personal attention, and enjoy a delicious heartland breakfast along the shores of Madison's largest lake.
    Each of the rooms at the Middleton Beach Inn has a unique quality and charm. We use soft linens, hand stitched quilts, oversized towels, and down pillows. Each guest is invited to walk down and enjoy the area's largest athletic facility—The Harbor Athletic Club—as our guest.

Raspberry Stuffed French Toast

serves 4-6

Ingredients:

1 — 1 pound loaf unsliced old fashioned bread
1 cup raspberry pie filling (other fillings may be substituted)
6 large eggs
1 cup milk
1 teaspoon vanilla
1/2 teaspoon ground cinnamon
Dash of nutmeg
Powdered sugar
Whipped cream topping
Fresh raspberries

Procedure:

Slice bread into 1 1/4" slices with a serrated bread knife. Carefully cut a pocket starting at the top crust of each slice almost to the bottom.

In a mixing bowl, beat eggs, vanilla, milk, cinnamon and nutmeg until combined. Warm raspberry filling and spoon into pockets (approximately 3 teaspoons each slice). Close pockets and gently shift mixture evenly inside bread. Dip stuffed pockets into egg mixture being careful not to let bread get over saturated (10 seconds each side). Cook on coated skillet or griddle at medium heat until golden brown on each side.

Sprinkle with powdered sugar and garnish with whipped cream topping and fresh raspberries. Can be served with fresh maple or apple syrup.

Room rates at the Middleton Beach Inn range from $65-$125, which include a full breakfast.

The Mustard Seed Bed and Breakfast

205 California Avenue, P.O. Box 262, Hayward, WI 54843
715•634•2908

Hosts: Betty and Jim Teske

Enjoy Scandinavian hospitality—country ambiance in our 100 year old lumberman's home. Walking distance to historic downtown Hayward. Easy access to trails—mountain bike, ski, hike or canoe, then, relax by the fireplace. The inn is air conditioned and has whirlpool tubs.

"Where you will arrive a stranger, but will depart a friend."

Norwegian Sour Cream Waffles with Apple Pecan Topping

serves 4

Ingredients:

2 cups sour cream
2 fresh eggs
1 cup unbleached flour
1 teaspoon baking powder
1/2 teaspoon baking soda
1/2 teaspoon salt
2 tablespoons sugar
1/2 teaspoon ground cardamon
3 tablespoons water

APPLE PECAN TOPPING:
2 tablespoons butter
1/4 cup brown sugar
2 large apples cored and sliced
1/4 cup chopped pecans
1/2 teaspoon cinnamon

Procedure:

In large bowl beat sour cream until fluffy. In separate bowl beat eggs until light, combine with sour cream and beat again. Sift dry ingredients, fold into sour cream/egg mixture—add water. Bake, according to wafflemaker directions. Serve with maple syrup and apple pecan topping.

APPLE PECAN TOPPING:
In skillet melt butter and brown sugar. Add apples, cinnamon and pecans. Cook until apples are tender—about 3-4 minutes. Keep warm.

Rates at The Mustard Seed range from $50-$80 per night, which include a full breakfast.

The Nash House—A Bed & Breakfast

1020 Oak Street, Wisconsin Rapids, WI 54494
715•424•2001

Hosts: Phyllis and Jim Custer

Rest warm in winter in queen beds under down comforters. In summer enjoy ceiling fans or air conditioning (though it is hardly ever needed).

Eat a delicious breakfast in the dining room or on the screened porch. You may find one of the recipes in this book made for your enjoyment.

Soak in the footed bathtubs, dally on our porch swing, nap in the hammock, stroll the neighborhood, cozy up to the living room fireplace.

Take time to enjoy the local sites and activities. We have historical and industrial places to see, nature preserves to hike, excellent restaurants for dining. You may use our tandem bicycle to help you explore.

Marion's Danish Pastry

serves 8

Ingredients:

PASTRY:
1 cup flour
1/2 cup butter
2 tablespoons water

TOPPING:
1/2 cup butter
  boiled with:
1 cup water
1 cup flour
3 eggs
1 teaspoon almond flavoring

FROSTING:
1 1/2 cups powdered sugar
2 tablespoons butter
1 1/2 teaspoons almond or vanilla flavoring
1-2 tablespoons water

Procedure:

PASTRY:
   Mix flour, butter and water as for pastry. Round into ball and divide in half. Roll each half into 12" x 3" strips. Place on greased cookie sheets.

TOPPING:
   Boil water and butter. Add flour stirring fast. Add eggs, one at a time, beating until smooth. Stir in almond flavoring.
   Spoon onto crusts and bake one hour at 350°.

FROSTING:
   Mix powdered sugar, butter, almond of vanilla flavoring and water until smooth. Frost pastry when cool.

Rates at the Nash House range from $40-$45, which include a full breakfast.

The Night Heron

315 E. Water Street, Cambridge-Rockdale, WI 53523
608•423•4141

Host: Pam Schorr and John Lehman

The drive isn't far, just long enough to put the stress of work, demands of children or deadlines of school behind you. This is the "getting away from it all" you've been promising yourself . . . a chance to kindle that flame of romance with someone you appreciate and love.

The Night Heron provides the complimentary refreshments, hot tub, old fashioned terry cloth robes, down-covered queen size beds and your choice of three enchanting, very reasonable, very romantic rooms. You're across from the beautiful Koshkonong river and hiking trails through 300 acres of nature parks. The two of you can bike to neighboring Cambridge—nationally known for its hand crafted pottery. We'll even provide the bikes. And, at night chose from a variety of country restaurant "finds."

In the morning sit on the umbrella terrace and let us serve you a leisurely breakfast of fruit, Pam's famous quiche, fresh baked goods and custom blended coffees. Take your time. Perhaps, check out some antique shops on your way back home.

Experience the Night Heron Bed and Breakfast. Cozy, comfortable and especially romantic. The smiles and memories will last for a long time afterwards.

Pam's Southwestern Spicy Quiche

makes three quiches (four servings each)

Ingredients:

1 1/2 pounds bacon—crisply fried and crumbled
1 cup chopped onions
2 cups shredded hot pepper cheese
2 cups shredded cheddar cheese
10 eggs beaten
2 cups half-and-half
2 teaspoons white pepper
1 small can tomatoes—chopped and drained
3 deep dish Ritz pie shells

Procedure:

Fry bacon. Leave 1 tablespoon bacon grease remaining to saute onions, add tomatoes. In a large bowl beat eggs, add half-and-half, white pepper and mix together. In another large bowl mix together cheeses, onions, tomatoes and bacon. Arrange into pie shells evenly. Pour eggs and cream mixture over cheese.

Wrap in tin foil and freeze. Take out a day before and set in refrigerator to thaw. Bake at 375° for 1 hour. Let cool for 10 minutes, cut into quarters and serve.

This spicy blend of cheeses will awaken the palate and put zest into your guests' morning. It will also allow you an extra half hour sleep.

I like to serve this with fresh fruit and croissants.

Rates at the Night Heron range from $50-$65, which include a full breakfast.

Oak Hill Manor

401 E. Main Street, Albany, WI 53502
608•862•1400

Hosts: Lee and Mary DeWolf

Seated on an acre of gardens, summer at Oak Hill Manor brings an abundance of black raspberries which we love to turn into jam, and fall brings a harvest of black walnuts. They add the distinctive flavor to our walnut fudge waffles, which we serve piping hot with baked eggs and grilled sausage patties, fresh fruits and juices, and, of course, a selection of famous Green County cheeses.

Summer days start with early morning coffee on the porch overlooking the flower gardens and winter breakfasts are served by the fireplace.

Our home is decorated and furnished as it would have been at the turn of the century. The four spacious guest rooms are air-conditioned and all have private baths.

If the bounty of your breakfast is as important as the beauty of your bedroom, visit us at Oak Hill Manor.

Black Walnut Fudge Waffles

5 waffles

Ingredients:

6 tablespoons butter flavored shortening
6 tablespoons Hershey's cocoa
3 eggs
3/4 cup flour
1/2 cup milk
1 teaspoon baking powder
1/2 teaspoon salt
1/2 cup sugar
1/8 teaspoon baking soda
1 teaspoon vanilla
1/2 cup black walnuts, chopped fine

Procedure:

    With a wire whisk, blend the cocoa into the shortening. Whisk eggs into shortening and do the same with the milk. Sift together flour, baking powder, soda, salt and sugar. With a spoon, beat dry ingredients into shortening mixture. Stir in vanilla and nuts. Bake waffles, in a hot iron, just until they stop steaming.
    We serve these waffles with our homemade black raspberry jam, or they are extra good with a dollop of ice cream and hot fudge topping.

Room rates at the Oak Hill Manor are $55, which include a full breakfast.

Old Rittenhouse Inn

301 Rittenhouse Avenue, P.O. Box 584, Bayfield, WI 54814
715•779•5111

Hosts: Mary and Jerry Phillips

The Old Rittenhouse Inn is located in Bayfield, Wisconsin on the shore of Lake Superior. The Inn offers Victorian lodging and elegant dining. Twenty-one guest rooms are located in three historic homes. Each guest room is furnished with antiques, private baths and all but one have working fireplaces. Suites and rooms with whirlpools and lake views are available.

Dining is offered nightly to the public. The leisurely paced five course meal features a verbally presented menu and regional specialties. Dinner is a fixed price of $35 per person. Group luncheons, weddings and business meetings can be arranged by advance reservations.

Wild Blueberry Scones with Blueberry Sauce

10-12 3" scones

Ingredients:

SCONES:
1 1/2 cups unbleached all-purpose flour
1/2 teaspoon baking soda
1 teaspoon cream of tartar
1/8 teaspoon salt
1 medium egg, lightly beaten
1 1/4 cups milk
1 tablespoon sugar
1/2 cup blueberries

BLUEBERRY SAUCE:
1 cup fresh blueberries
   (Domestic blueberries may be substituted)
2 tablespoons lemon juice
1 1/2 cups sugar
Grated peel of one lemon

Procedure:

SCONES:
   Sift together flour, baking soda, cream of tartar, and salt.
   In a separate bowl, mix egg, milk, and sugar. Slowly add this to flour mixture until the batter is thick. Pour 1/3 cup of batter for each scone onto a hot, lightly greased griddle. Drop blueberries onto each scone.
   When bubbles appear on top of the scone, flip it over. Serve with butter and warm blueberry sauce.

SAUCE:
   Blend blueberries and lemon juice. Fold in sugar and lemon peel. Heat to boiling point stirring continually.
   Serve with scones.

Room rates at the Old Rittenhouse Inn range from $99 to $189 and include complimentary continental breakfast. Full breakfast is available for an additional charge.

Parkview Bed and Breakfast

211 N. Park Street, Reedsburg, WI 53959-1652
608•524•4333

Hosts: Tom and Donna Hofmann

    Fishponds, a windmill, and lighthouse made of stones and shells are the legacy left by the second owner of this 1895 Queen Anne Victorian home located a block from the business district in Reedsburg's Historic District across from City Park. A two-room playhouse, original to the property, delights the younger guests. The home features original woodwork, beveled and etched windows, a built-in buffet, and a suitor's window. The Hofmann family has done most of the work in the restoration of the inside and outside of the home and work together in the operation of the business.
    Guests enjoy wake-up coffee outside their bedrooms. Donna, a home economist, plans the full breakfast menu after talking with guests to learn their preferences and any special restrictions they may have. The menus are varied and reflect the season of the year.
    Parkview is conveniently located near Wisconsin Dells, Baraboo, and Spring Green. The new 400 Bike Trail that connects to the Elroy/Sparta Trail is just three blocks away.

Blueberry Buttermilk Muffins

makes 14-18 muffins

Ingredients:

2 1/2 cups flour
2 1/2 teaspoons baking powder
1 cup sugar
1/4 teaspoon salt
1 cup buttermilk
2 eggs, beaten
1/4 pound butter, melted and lightly browned
1 1/2 cups blueberries

Procedure:

Sift dry ingredients together into large bowl. Make a well; add buttermilk, eggs, and melted, brown butter. Mix well. Fold in blueberries. Bake in well-greased muffins tins at 375°F for 20 minutes or until brown. Serve warm.

Rates at the Parkview range from $45-$65, which include a full breakfast.

Pederson Victorian Bed & Breakfast

Route 5, Box 833, 1782 Highway 120 North, Lake Geneva, WI 53147
414•248•9110

Hostess: Kristi Cowles

Let's see . . . there's 1880 authenticity with white gingerbread trim, a front porch swing, original hanging lights, stained glass, a cozy parlor and a delightful sunroom.

What else . . . how about four lovely bedrooms (one with a private bath and three that share) and the "fresh-air fragrance" of line-dried sheets . . . even in winter (honest!). An upstairs bathroom that will knock your socks off with "old clawfoot" right smack dab in the middle; "wonderful-for-your-skin" bath products, including green mineral bath oil that really soothes aching bones and muscles.

Plus . . . full, vegetarian breakfasts. Bicycle storage and backyard hammocks. Every kind of recreational activity imaginable, including quiet back country roads for bicycling, walking, smooching and an innkeeper that is obviously an incurable romantic . . . and sometimes . . . even a red tail hawk!

So, come for a visit, already.

Feta Vegie Quiche
With Rolled Oat and Wheat Germ Crust

serves 8-10

Ingredients:

CRUST:
2 cups whole-grain bread crumbs
1 cup wheat germ
1 cup rolled oats
1/2 cup whole wheat flour
1 cup olive oil (or melted butter)
Dashes of marjoram or basil

FILLING:
12 "farm fresh" eggs
1 cup plain yogurt or sour cream
1 cup milk
3 cups sliced Vegies (your favorite combinations)
1 cup jack or raw milk cheddar cheese, grated (feta)
1-2 teaspoons basil, marjoram, tarragon or dill (combined)
1 teaspoon garlic salt
Pepper to taste
Paprika

Procedure:

CRUST:
Mix all ingredients except olive oil together. Add oil. Mix with fork and press into a buttered 9" x 13" pan. Bake at 400° for 10 minutes. Remove and fill with cheese and egg mixture.

FILLING:
Beat eggs, yogurt, milk, herbs and spices together. Saute vegies in small amount olive oil and add to mixture. Crumble feta and grated cheese onto crust. Pour egg mixture over cheeses. Sprinkle with paprika. Bake at 350° for one hour.

These recipes can be halved and baked in a 9" round pie pan at 350° for 45 minutes.

I serve this quiche with whole-wheat English muffins, topped with butter, parmesan cheese, garlic salt and/or basil, and placed under a broiler for four minutes, fresh fruit, juices and organic coffee. Typical guest comments are as follows: Mmmmmmmmm. Ooooooo. Wowwwwww. Nuuuuummmmmm.

Rates at Pederson Victorian Bed and Breakfast range from $42-$75 per night, which include a full, vegetarian breakfast.

Phipps Inn

1005 3rd Street, Hudson, WI 54016
715•386•0800

Hosts: Cyndi and John Berglund

This romantic 1884 Queen Anne Victorian Inn is located in historic Hudson, a river town nestled along the scenic St. Croix, yet, only 20 minutes from the St. Paul/Minneapolis area.

The Inn offers three parlors and a formal dining room on the first floor and six suites, most with whirlpools and fireplaces on the second and third floors.

A lavish and leisurely four course breakfast is served in the dining room or is served in your suite on weekends, with a lighter fare served during the week.

Nearby attractions include the Octagon House, the Phipps Theatre, St. Croix River, Willow River State Park, hot air ballooning, shopping and fine dining.

Step through our door and back across one hundred years into a more graceful era . . .

Cherry-Berry Meringue Shortcakes

makes 4

Ingredients:

2 egg whites
1/2 teaspoon vanilla extract
1/4 teaspoon cream of tartar
1/3 cup sugar
4 round angel food cake cups
1/2 cup fresh raspberries
1/2 cup pitted halved fresh dark cherries
1/2 cup lemon yogurt
1/4 cup whipped topping

Procedure:

Preheat oven to 450°. Grease baking sheet; set aside. In medium bowl, beat egg whites, vanilla and cream of tartar with electric mixer on high until soft peaks form. Gradually add sugar, beating until stiff peaks form.

Place cake cups on greased cookie sheet. Spread meringue over each cake, building up sides to hold fruit. Bake 5-6 minutes or until golden brown. Place on rack to cool.

Fill centers of cake with raspberries and cherries. In small bowl, fold together yogurt and whipped topping. Spoon over fruit.

Rates at the Phipps Inn range from $100-$180, which include a full breakfast.

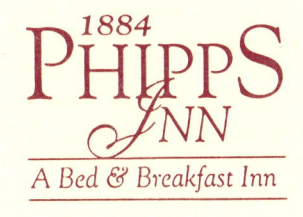

1884 Phipps Inn
A Bed & Breakfast Inn

Pinehaven Bed and Breakfast

E13083 Highway 33, Baraboo, WI 53913
608•356•3489

Hosts: Lyle and Marge Getschman

Come to the country and we will share our beautiful view with you, and make you feel at home in our home. Enjoy our small private lake with the Baraboo bluffs in the background. Four air conditioned rooms with private baths and queen or twin beds. Ask about our private Guest House.

Potato Broccoli Quiche

serves 8

Ingredients:

1 — 24 ounce package Ore Ida O'Brian frozen potatoes, thawed
1/2 cup fresh broccoli (partly cooked)
1/2 cup cheddar cheese (cubed)
3/4 cup ham (cubed)
5 eggs (beaten)
1 cup milk
1/4 teaspoon salt
Pepper to taste
3/4 cup cheddar cheese, shredded

Procedure:

Press thawed potatoes into 7" x 11" baking dish. Sprinkle with salt and pepper if desired. Add broccoli, cheese and ham cubes. Mix beaten eggs and milk and pour over other ingredients. Bake at 350° for 40 minutes. Top with shredded cheese and bake 10 more minutes.

Rates at Pinehaven range from $60-$95 per night, which include a full breakfast.

Pleasant Lake Inn

2238 60th Avenue, Osceola, WI 54020-4509
715•294•2545

Hosts: Richard and Charlene Berg

    Although Pleasant Lake Inn is a new country style home built on a small, quiet lake, it brings with it a lot of history.
    Adjacent to the bed and breakfast, is an operating dairy farm that has been in the family since 1857. The fifth generation is now living in the original farm house.
    The bed and breakfast offers three spacious rooms, all with private baths—two with double whirlpools and private decks overlooking the lake. The third room has a large enclosed sun room overlooking the lake. Open year round.

Honey Baked French Toast

serves 6-8

Ingredients:

15 slices of diagonally cut French or Italian bread
4 large eggs
1 1/2 cups milk
4 tablespoons honey
3 tablespoons brown sugar
2 tablespoons melted butter
2 teaspoons cinnamon

Procedure:

Grease a 9" x 13" pan. In a large bowl, lightly beat eggs with 2 tablespoons of honey and the cinnamon. Add the milk and mix well. Dip the bread slices in the mixture. Arrange three rows of five slices each, overlapping slices slightly. Pour any remaining egg mixture over the slices. Cover and refrigerate overnight. In morning, preheat oven to 350°. Sprinkle with 3 tablespoons brown sugar. Drizzle with 2 remaining tablespoons honey and the melted butter. Bake for 30 minutes.

Rates at Pleasant Lake range from $70-$90 for Friday-Saturday, and $50-$75 for Sunday-Thursday. All include a full breakfast.

Port Washington's Inn

308 W. Washington, Port Washington, WI 53074
414•284•5583

Hosts: Robert and Kimberly Mueller

The Port Washington's Inn was built by a prominent brew master during the turn-of-the-century. Our home features original stained glass, leaded glass, oak woodwork, large guest chambers and antiques throughout. Tucked away on top of Sweetcake Hill with views of Lake Michigan and the Art Deco Lighthouse. Short distance to marina and downtown, where you will find the best restaurants around and quaint shops. Other area attractions include Cedarburg, Herrington Beach State Park, Kettle Moraine, and only 30 minutes north of Milwaukee.

Grandma's Morning Muffins

about 2 dozen

Ingredients:

6 eggs
1 1/2 cups oil
1 teaspoon vanilla
2 1/4 cups sugar
4 cups flour
4 teaspoons baking soda
1 teaspoon salt
3 teaspoons cinnamon
1 cup raisins
1 cup coconut
4 cups shredded carrots
2 large apples, shredded
1/2 cups nuts (optional)

Procedure:

Mix eggs, oil and vanilla together. Add dry ingredients to egg mixture; stir. Then fold in the fruits and carrots. Pour into greased muffin pans. Bake at 375° for 20 minutes. Muffins are moist and freeze wonderfully.

Rates at Port Washington's Inn range from $55-$95, which include a full breakfast.

The Queen Anne Bed and Breakfast

837 E. College Avenue, Appleton, WI 54911
414•739•7966

Hosts: Susan and Larry Bogenschutz

Edna Ferber and Harry Houdini are noted personalities of this Appleton neighborhood. The world's most extensive exhibit of Houdini's memorabilia is on display at the Houdini Historical Center which is within walking distance of this authentically restored and decorated 1890s Victorian home.

Gracious hosts await your arrival and invite you to relax and enjoy the ambiance of times gone by in this meticulously restored Queen Anne.

Throughout the home, guests take pleasure in touches of another era. From the grand foyer to the parlors which feature working fireplaces to the bedrooms which are appointed with sumptuous antique furnishings and beds piled high with down quilts and pillows, guests are treated to a luxurious and relaxing stay.

Beckoned to the dining room by the aroma of freshly brewed coffee and warm muffins, guests linger over a full breakfast prepared and served by friendly hosts.

Reservations required. Please write or call.

Queen Anne's Crepes Asparagus Cordon Bleu

4-6 servings

Ingredients:

BASIC CREPES:
5 eggs
2 1/3 cups milk
2 cups sifted flour
3 tablespoons vegetable oil
1/4 teaspoon salt

FILLING:
1 1/2 pounds fresh asparagus
    spears
8 thick slices cooked ham
Dijon mustard
8 slices Swiss cheese
2 tomatoes, peeled and chopped
Dried parsley
Tarragon

SAUCE:
3 tablespoons butter or margarine
3 tablespoons flour
1/2 teaspoon each of salt
    and tarragon (crushed)
Pepper
1 1/2 cups half-and-half
1 (2 1/2 ounce) jar sliced
    mushrooms (optional)

Procedure:

To prepare crepes, beat eggs with electric mixer on medium speed in a large bowl until well beaten. Add milk, flour, oil and salt. Beat with electric mixer on medium speed until batter is smooth. Cover and refrigerate 2-3 hours. Preheat small, shallow skillet (or crepe pan); brush with oil if necessary. Using 2 to 4 tablespoons batter for each crepe, cook on preheated pan over medium-high heat 2 to 3 minutes or until underside is lightly browned. To remove crepe, loosen edges and gently lift crepe with spatula. Stack between waxed paper for easy freezing and separation. Makes 30 to 40 crepes.

Preheat oven to 375°F. Trim asparagus. In large pan, cook asparagus spears in boiling salted water until crisp-tender; drain. Place a slice of ham on each crepe. Spread ham slice with mustard. Top with slice of cheese, asparagus spears, and chopped tomatoes. Sprinkle with dried parsley and tarragon. Roll crepes, placing seam-side down in a 13" x 9" baking dish.

To prepare sauce, melt butter or margarine in medium saucepan. Blend in flour, 1/2 teaspoon tarragon, salt and pepper. Stir in half-and-half. Stir constantly over medium-high heat until thick and bubbly. Stir in mushrooms. Pour sauce over crepes in baking dish.

Bake 25 minutes or until heated through. Serve warm. ENJOY!

Rates at the Queen Anne range from $60-$85 per night, which include a full breakfast.

Red Forest Bed and Breakfast

1421 25th Street, Two Rivers, WI 54241
414•793•1794

Hosts: Kay and Alan Rodewald

The Family Rodewald warmly welcomes you to step back in time to 1907 and enjoy the Red Forest Bed and Breakfast. Red Forest being the English translation of our German name Rodewald. Our German heritage and old world charm is gently blended into our comfortable home. From the trophy deer mounts by the fireplace, to Great Grandparents' family wedding pictures in "Granny's Sewing Room," to the German Apple Pancake served with homemade maple syrup to our guests in the morning.

Two Rivers is located on Wisconsin's East Coast on the sun-spangled shores of Lake Michigan, midway from Chicago to the Door County peninsula.

Baked German Apple Pancake

serves 4-6

Ingredients:

1/4 cup flour
1/4 cup milk
Dash of salt
3 eggs, separated
2 tablespoons margarine
1/2 cup sugar
1 teaspoon cinnamon
3 large or 4 small Granny Smith apples, peeled, cored
    and sliced 1/4 inch thick.

Procedure:

Preheat oven 350°. Place 9" ovenproof glass pie dish with deep sides in preheated oven.

Beat egg whites until stiff. Mix flour, milk, salt and egg yolks in separate bowl with hand mixer. Then gently fold egg white mixture in.

Saute apples, sugar, margarine and cinnamon in skillet for 2-3 minutes until apples are well coated.

Pour apples into heated glass pie dish sprayed with non-stick cooking spray. Pour the batter over apple slices. Bake for 20 minutes at 350° until the pancake is brown and puffy.

Remove from oven and loosen sides. Place a round plate over glass pie dish and flip over. Cut the pancake in wedges and serve with maple syrup.

Before opening our Bed and Breakfast, I tried several different breakfast recipes. I tried this recipe for our family Easter Brunch. It was an instant favorite, and a favorite of our guests ever since.

Rates at the Red Forest are $55-$75, which include a full breakfast.

River Terrace Bed and Breakfast

521 River Terrace, Kiel, WI 53042
414•894•2032

Hosts: Jim and Barbara Fett

Built in 1891 by a local lumber supplier as a wedding present to his wife, the large estate is located in the heart of Kiel in Manitowoc County. The house contains hardwood floors, original woodwork and wallcoverings that typify the Victorian splendor of the late 1800's. Most unique are the "art deco" stained glass fixtures in the living room. Guests at River Terrace are within walking distance of shopping areas and the running path that connects several of the city parks. Kiel is a short distance from many summer events including Road America, E.A.A. and Walleye Weekend. Local activities include the Black Wolf Run Golf Course at Kohler, the Kettle Moraine ski trails and the Wade House at Greenbush. A gregarious sheepdog welcomes guests to River Terrace which is open year round.

Fiesta River Terrace

serves 6

Ingredients:

3 tablespoons butter or margarine
2 cups diced uncooked potatoes (about 3 medium)
1 cup finely chopped onions
1/2 cup finely crumbled cooked Italian sausage
1 can (4 ounce) chopped green chilies
1 tablespoon chopped fresh cilantro or 1/4 cup chopped parsley
6 eggs
1/4 teaspoon salt
2 tablespoons milk
1/2 cup shredded Monterey Jack cheese
Bottled taco or picante sauce

Procedure:

    In a 10" ovenproof skillet, melt butter or margarine. Add potatoes and onions; cover and cook over medium-low heat 20 minutes or until potatoes are golden and tender, stirring occasionally.
    Add sausage, chilies and cilantro or parsley; cook 2 minutes. Reduce heat.
    Preheat oven to 350°F. In a small bowl beat eggs, salt, and milk until well blended. Pour eggs over potato mixture. Cover and bake for 20 minutes or until eggs are set. Sprinkle cheese on top and bake covered, another 5 minutes.
    Serve with sauce.

Rates at River Terrace range from $45-$50, which include a continental plus breakfast.

Rose Ivy Inn

228 South Watertown Street, Waupun, WI 53963
414•324•2127 or 800•258•5019

Hosts: Melody and Ken Kris

The Rose Ivy Inn is nestled in the peaceful, historic city of Waupun, "Wild Goose Center" of Wisconsin. A short distance from the Inn is the Horicon Marsh Wildlife Refuge where each spring and fall thousands of Canadian geese migrate to the marshland haven creating a spectacular sight. The Refuge offers great hiking, birding, walking, biking, and cross-country skiing.

The Rose Ivy Inn is a romantic, Queen Anne Victorian home filled with lace, antiques, and the fragrance of roses. Built in 1900, it still echoes the ambience of a by-gone era with its beautiful oak foyer, ornate fireplace, and gleaming hardwood floors. Each of the four guest rooms is graced with the name of an Old Garden Rose, and is furnished in elegant and inviting Victorian antiques intertwined tastefully with today's comforts.

Breakfast is a special time at the Inn, and is served either in the elegant dining room or, on warm days, the curved porch overlooking the Victorian rose garden.

Relax and enjoy time away from the hectic pace of everyday life at the Rose Ivy Inn where guest comfort is of utmost importance.

Grandmother's Famous Cranberry Bread

1 large loaf or 3 mini-loaves

Ingredients:

2 cups sifted all-purpose flour
1 cup white sugar
1 1/2 teaspoons baking powder
1 teaspoon salt
1/2 teaspoon baking soda
1/4 cup butter
1 egg, beaten
1 teaspoon grated orange peel
3/4 cup orange juice (either fresh-squeezed or frozen)
3 cups fresh cranberries, halved
1 cup coarsely chopped walnuts

Procedure:

Sift flour, sugar, baking powder, salt, and baking soda into a large bowl. Cut in butter until mixture is crumbly. Add egg, orange peel, and orange juice all at once; stir just until mixture is evenly moist. Fold in cranberries and nuts.

Spoon into a greased 9" x 5" x 3" loaf pan or 3 greased mini-loaf pans. Bake at 350° for 1 hour and 10 minutes for large loaf, 40 minutes for mini loaves, or until toothpick comes out clean. Remove from pan, cool on a wire rack.

Best if eaten day after baking. Freezes well, too.

(This tasty cranberry bread recipe really isn't a treasured recipe from Grandma! It actually comes from a treasured storybook read to our children when they were very young! Nearly twenty years ago they asked me to try this recipe, and I've been using it ever since.)

Rates at the Rose Ivy range from $59-$79, which include a full breakfast.

The Scofield House Bed and Breakfast

908 Michigan Street, Sturgeon Bay (Door County), WI 54235-1849
414•743•7727

Hosts: Bill and Fran Cecil

"Door County's most elegant bed and breakfast," or so it has been called by many travel writers, and featured in many national magazines. This 1902 multi-colored, 3 story Victorian, once Mayor Scofield's ornate home, was bought and restored by Bill and Fran Cecil in January of 1987. Bill was a health care executive, and Fran a nurse executive looking for "something to do with their lives." That winter day in Door County they "made the wrong turn and the right decision" when they saw the house for sale. Bill is the chef/innkeeper and keeps the guests coming back for his wonderful gourmet breakfasts. Fran bakes the homemade cookies and "sweet treats" served fresh every afternoon with teas and gourmet coffees. Breakfasts vary daily and include fresh and baked seasonal fruit dishes, fresh muffins, and entrees like Eggs Benedict, fancy omelets, cherry and pecan pancakes, and more.

The Scofield House has six guest rooms, of which four are suites, all with private bath, color tv/vcr, and a "free" video library. Double whirlpools, fireplaces, and central A/C. Smoke free environment. No children please. Open all year.

Scofield House Egg and Sausage Strata

serves 10-12

Ingredients:

2 pounds bulk pork sausage
8 ounces sour cream
6 whole English muffins (sour dough, whole wheat, plain)
1 pound grated Monterey Jack cheese
6 extra large eggs
2 1/2 cups milk (2% or skim)
1 can condensed cream of mushroom soup
1 cup finely grated green pepper (optional)

Procedure:

Brown and drain pork sausage. Mix soup and sour cream together. Crumble muffins and line a greased 9" x 13" baking pan. Mix eggs and milk together in a separate bowl. Layer in pan 1/2 sausage, 1/2 grated cheese, 1/2 soup mixture onto crumbled muffins. Repeat layers ending with soup mixture, then smooth with spatula. Pour milk and egg mixture over all (poke with sharp knife to help absorb milk mixture). Wrap with plastic and foil and refrigerate overnight. Next day bake uncovered at 300° for 1 hour. "Rest" on rack for 5 minutes. Cut into squares and serve. "Very rich, very delicious, a big favorite of guests," Bill Cecil. Reheats and freezes well.

Note: We usually double recipe and make two at a time and freeze one for later.

Rates at the Scofield House range from $69-$180 per night, which include a full breakfast.

Spider Lake Lodge Bed and Breakfast

Route 1, Box 1335, Hayward, WI 54843
715•462•3793 or 800•OLD•WISC

Hosts: Min, Paul and Barbara Grossi

Our guests tell us this is what they had always imagined a Northern Wisconsin log lodge to be. Built of hand-hewn tamarack logs by the proud craftsmen of 1923, this grand old lodge on Spider Lake invites you to step back to a simpler, relaxing time. To entire days spent out in the clear country air, of hearty appetites and full fireside breakfasts, of summer breezes and moonlight on the lake from the screen porch, cool evenings spent by a crackling fire, and falling asleep to the crickets song or the winter silence. The lodge has spacious dining and sitting areas, huge stone fireplaces, and cozy, unique guest rooms decorated with many of the original furnishings. All have private baths. We're footsteps from the lake, and minutes to golf, biking, or skiing the Birkebeiner and other fine area trail systems.

Patty's Fireside Pumpkin Bread

Makes 1 large or 2 small loaves

Ingredients:

1/2 cup sugar
1/2 cup Wesson oil
2 eggs
1 cup canned pumpkin
1 3/4 cups flour
1/4 teaspoon baking powder
1 teaspoon soda
1 teaspoon salt
1/2 teaspoon ground cloves
3/4 teaspoon cinnamon
1/2 teaspoon nutmeg
1/2 teaspoon allspice
1/3 cup water
1/2 cup raisins
1/2 cup or to taste chopped walnuts

Procedure:

Preheat oven to 350°. Add sugar to oil, then add eggs, and pumpkin. Next add spices sifted with flour then the water, then raisins and nuts. Bake at 350° for 1 hour. Makes 1 large or 2 small loaves. This bread freezes exceptionally well.

Rates at the Spider Lake Lodge range from $60-$85 per night, which include a full breakfast.

Sugar River Inn Bed and Breakfast

304 S. Mill Street, Albany, WI 53502
608•862•1248

Hosts: Jack and Ruth Lindberg

In years past our turn of the century home hosted the town parties and formal dinners. The charm of the home still says "welcome" today with its warm and comfortable decor.

Enjoy the spacious yard, the peacefulness of rural Wisconsin, and the exciting examples of nature you will find living in or near the river.

Four guest rooms, private and shared bath. Other attractions include a bike trail and canoeing on the river.

Wake up coffee and afternoon refreshments are served. Relax and take a slower pace of life.

Hospitality is an art that still lives here.

Golden Treat

serves 1

Ingredients:

3 tablespoons 100% natural oat cereal with almonds or coconut
2 tablespoons bran flakes
1 1/2 tablespoons golden raisins
1/4 fresh banana, diced

TOPPING:
2 tablespoons Dannon Vanilla Yogurt
1 tablespoon honey

Procedure:

Layer the ingredients in order in a long stemmed goblet or dessert dish. Cover with yogurt and drizzle with honey.

We serve "Golden Treat" first with juice and coffee, a side dish of fresh fruit, and a warm muffin. Then we complete our breakfast with an entree of blueberry pancakes with fresh blueberry sauce or French toast served with fresh cranberry sauce—a big hit!

Rates at the Sugar River Inn range from $55-$65 per night, which include a full breakfast.

Summit Farm Bed and Breakfast

1622 110 Avenue, Hammond, WI 54015
715•796•2617

Hosts: Grant and Laura Fritsche

An 80-year-old home nestled in a quiet farm community. Antique filled bedrooms, hearty breakfasts, sheep and ducks make us a true country experience. Pleasant lodgings down a quiet country lane.

Picante Sauce

5 pints

Ingredients:

2-3 small green chili peppers
7 sweet banana peppers
7 green or red bell peppers
6 large tomatoes
6 onions
1 tablespoon mustard seed
1/3 cup sugar
2 tablespoons salt
1/4 cup vinegar
1/2 cup ketchup

Procedure:

    Blanch tomatoes, remove skins and quarter. Chop or blend cut up peppers and onions with tomatoes and vinegar. (Wear gloves for hot peppers.)
    Place in large, heavy pan with remaining ingredients and boil 30 minutes stirring frequently to prevent burning.
    To can: Have sauce boiling. Pour immediately into hot jars that have been boiled. Put lids on tightly. They should seal on their own in one hour.

Rates at Summitt Farm range from $45-$60 per night, which include a full breakfast.

The Swallow's Nest Bed and Breakfast

141 Sarrington, P.O. Box 418, Lake Delton, WI 53940
608•254•6900

Hosts: Mary Ann and Rod Stemo

Visit our new home in a secluded setting located one mile off Interstate 90 and 94. Choose from four guest rooms, all with private baths and air conditioning. The home features monastery windows, two story atrium with skylights, a library with fireplace, and decks overlooking the lake. The home is furnished with family antiques and lace curtains from England. Play a game of pool, enjoy the photography studio and gallery which are on the premises. Artist is in residence. Recreation activities include: water sports, bike trail, cross country skiing, museum nature area, historical site, Devils Lake and Mirror Lake State parks near by and golfing. Open all year.

Whole Wheat Buttermilk Waffles

6-8 waffles

Ingredients:

3/4 cup whole wheat flour
3/4 cup all purpose flour
2 teaspoons baking powder
3/4 teaspoon baking soda
1/2 teaspoon salt
2 tablespoons sugar
3 eggs
1 1/2 cups buttermilk
3/4 cup (1 1/2 sticks) butter melted
1/4 cup milk if needed

Procedure:

Put the flour into a mixing bowl and add the baking powder, baking soda, salt and sugar. Combine liquid and dry ingredients; stir with a fork to blend. In another mixing bowl, beat the eggs until well blended. Stir in the buttermilk and the melted butter (cooled off a little). Stir the mixture until well mixed—if the batter seems rather thick, add the 1/4 cup milk to thin it. The batter should flow from the spoon, not plop.

Bake in a hot waffle iron until crisp and golden. Serve hot.

These waffles are appealing because of their crispy, nutty, wheaty taste. The perfect complement is warm honey which becomes thin and pours like syrup when heated. Apple sauce adds a great touch to the waffles. Serve broiled bacon with the waffles.

Rates at The Swallow's Nest range from $60-$70 per night, which include a full breakfast.

Taylor House

210 East Iola Street, P.O. Box 101, Iola, WI 54945
715•445•2204

Hosts: Crystal and Richard Anderson

Taylor House was the first bed and breakfast in Waupaca County. The house was built at the turn of the century for Mr. and Mrs. E.M. Taylor and is still furnished with the Taylor family furniture. The home features an old-fashioned sitting room, a formal dining room, and four guest bedrooms.

At the present time each guest receives a homemade doll made by Richard's mother to remind them of their visit to Taylor House.

Spring Muffins

Makes 18-24 depending on size

Ingredients:

1 1/4 cups brown sugar
1/2 cup salad oil
1 egg
2 teaspoons vanilla
1 cup buttermilk
1 1/2 cups diced rhubarb
1/2 cup chopped walnuts
2 1/2 cups flour
1 teaspoon soda
1 teaspoon baking powder
1/2 teaspoon salt

TOPPING:
1 tablespoon butter or margarine, melted
1/3 cup sugar
1 teaspoon cinnamon

Procedure:

Combine brown sugar, salad oil, egg, vanilla, and buttermilk. Beat well. Stir in rhubarb and walnuts.
In a separate bowl combine flour, soda, baking powder, and salt. Stir in rhubarb mixture until well blended. Spoon batter into greased muffin cups.
Pour sugar mixture (topping) over filled cups and press lightly. Bake at 400° for 20-25 minutes.

Rates at the Taylor House range from $35-$60, which include a full breakfast.

Timm's Hill Bed and Breakfast

N2036 County Road C, Ogema, WI 54459
715•767•5288

Hosts: Joyce and Jim Summers

Enjoy a relaxing stay in our turn-of-the-century farmhouse. Experience the country comfort of down comforters, colorful quilts, golden oak furniture, white wicker, hardwood floors, lace curtains, and hearty breakfasts. Feast on homemade breads, rolls, and muffins fresh from the oven. Breakfast is served in the big farm kitchen where the windows and glass doors bring the beauty of the outdoors inside.

Our bed and breakfast is nestled in the hills that surround the highest point in Wisconsin, Timm's Hill. This area is an unspoiled paradise for nature lovers. Climb the observation tower for a breathtaking view of wooded hills and spring fed lakes. Hikers and mountain bikers will enjoy exploring the Timm's Hill Trail that is an extension of the Ice Age Trail. The blacktop road that winds through the hills is a favorite scenic route for bikers.

This is an area for all seasons. Spring bursts forth with beds of yellow and white daffodils in our yard. The woods are carpeted with wild flowers. Perhaps this area is best known for the spectacular show of colored leaves in the fall. The vibrant reds and golds of the sugar maple bring people flocking to the Timm's Hill observation tower. We invite you to come too!

Spinach Pie

1 - 10" or 2 - 8" pies

Ingredients:

1 1—10" or 2—8" pie crusts
2 packages (10 ounces each) frozen, chopped spinach
2 tablespoons butter
1/2 cup chopped onion
1 clove garlic, chopped fine
8 ounces or 2 cups grated mozzarella cheese
3 tablespoons butter
3 tablespoons flour
1 1/2 cups milk
1 1/4 teaspoons salt
1/4 teaspoon pepper
Dash nutmeg
Dash dill weed
6 eggs, well beaten

TOPPING:

Grated cheddar cheese (about 1/3 cup)
Slices of onion and tomato

Procedure:

Cook spinach as directed on package and press out water. Melt 2 tablespoons butter and saute onion and garlic. Stir this into the drained spinach. Mix in the mozzarella cheese.

Melt 3 tablespoons butter and stir in 3 tablespoons flour. Add milk and cook, stirring constantly until thick. Add the salt and pepper, nutmeg, and dill weed. Stir this into the spinach mixture. Then fold in the beaten eggs. Pour into unbaked pie shells. Bake at 350° for 45 to 60 minutes (depending on the size of pie shells). During the last 10 minutes of baking, sprinkle grated cheese on top and place slices of onion and tomato decoratively on top of pie.

This pie freezes well. It can be made ahead and reheated in the oven or in a microwave oven.

Rates at Timm's Hill range from $50-$60 (with full breakfast).

Trillium

Route #2, Box 121, La Farge, WI 54639
608•625•4492

Hostess: Rosanne Boyett

Trillium has been welcoming guests to the charming cottage for more than 10 years. Located on our diversified, organic farm there are many opportunities for guests to enjoy this rural setting in southwestern Wisconsin. Families are welcome and rates are by the number of adults, per day. Privacy in a cozy cottage in an active farming community; near rivers, bike trails, cheese factories, state parks, trout streams, and historic sites.

Plum Conserve

4 half-pints (or 4 cups)

Ingredients:

5 cups (about 2 pounds) fresh plums, sliced
2 cups honey
1/2 cup finely chopped, fresh lemon with peel
1 cup raisins
1/2 cup slivered almonds
4 half-pint jelly jars, with lids and rings,
    prepared for hot-water processing

Procedure:

In heavy Dutch oven, mix plums and honey. Mix in remaining ingredients except almonds. Bring to boil over medium-high heat. Cook 15-25 minutes (depending on juiciness of plums), stirring frequently until thickened and jam-like in texture. Remove from heat. Stir in almonds. Fill hot, sterilized half-pint jars to within 1/4 inch of top. Place lid on each jar. Screw bands on loosely; process 10 minutes in boiling-water bath. Remove from bath; tighten bands. Cool. Store in cupboard.

Excellent served with fresh, hot breads or toasted English muffins.

Rates at Trillium range from $60-$70. We also offer single rates, weekly rates and winter rates. Full breakfast included.

Trillium Woods Bed and Breakfast

N7453 910th Street, River Falls, WI 54022
715•425•2555

Hosts: Bobby and Milo Gray

Trillium Woods, our romantic Cape Cod home, welcomes you to a New England experience. Surrounded by magnificent maples and stately oaks, you will be enchanted by the beauty of a forest laden with hepatica, trillium, violets and fern, a meandering spring fed stream, and opportunities for hiking, bird watching, photography, and relaxation.

You will find loving touches in each of our private air conditioned Grandma Moses, Currier and Ives, and Charles Wysocki suites. Beautiful custom crafted Amish beds with hand stitched quilts, dust ruffles, and bed steps will offer you peaceful slumber. A knock on the door will bring you deliciously brewed fresh ground coffee to begin your morning and a full breakfast will summon you to the deck, three season porch, dining or fireside rooms.

We love to embellish the stay of our guests with surprises, perhaps a stream side picnic, birthday cake or lantern lighted evening hike.

Each season holds a magic all its own. We do maple sugaring in late winter and invite our guests to participate if they wish.

English Steamed Cranberry Pudding with Hard Sauce

10-12 servings

Ingredients:

1/2 cup shortening
2/3 cup sugar
2 beaten eggs
2 1/2 cups coarsely chopped fresh cranberries
2 tablespoons light molasses
1 2/3 cups sifted enriched flour
3/4 teaspoon soda
1/2 teaspoon cinnamon
1/4 teaspoon nutmeg
1/4 teaspoon salt

HARD SAUCE:
1 cup half and half cream
1 cup butter
2 cups sugar
1 teaspoon vanilla

Procedure:

Cream shortening and sugar; add eggs, cranberries, and molasses. Sift flour, soda, cinnamon, nutmeg, and salt together; add to the first mixture. Mix well.

Thoroughly grease 1 1/2-quart mold and dust lightly with flour; pour in batter. Cover tightly; steam about 3 1/2 hours.

HARD SAUCE:
Combine ingredients. Cook in double boiler until thick.

This is a Christmas brunch tradition in our home at Trillium Woods passed down from my grandmother Elizabeth Powers. It is easily doubled, keeps well for many days if refrigerated, and is beautiful served on a platter surrounded by sugar cubes soaked in brandy and set on fire. Excellent holiday dessert.

Our suite rates at Trillium Woods range from $65-$105, which include a full breakfast.

Ty-Bach

3104 Simpson Lane, Lac du Flambeau, WI 54538
715•588•7851

Hosts: Janet and Kermit Bekkum

Ty-Bach has a unique setting—being located on the Lac du Flambeau Chippewa Indian Reservation. Guests enjoy the quiet—punctuated by the songs of birds or the call of the loons. There are many interesting activities and attractions in the area. Our home is tastefully furnished and decorated. Each bedroom has a private bath.

Pears with Custard Sauce

serves 6

Ingredients:

PEARS:
1/2 cup water
2 tablespoons sugar
3 medium/large pears, peeled, quartered and cored
2 cinnamon sticks

CUSTARD SAUCE:
2 egg yolks, beaten
1/4 cup sugar
1/4 teaspoon salt
3/4 cup milk
1/4 cup evaporated milk
1 teaspoon vanilla

Procedure:

PEARS:
Combine water, sugar and cinnamon sticks in saucepan. Bring to boil. Add quartered pears. Reduce heat to low. Cover pan and simmer until pears are tender, about 20 minutes. Remove pears and place in dish. Return liquid to a boil and cook until syrupy. Remove cinnamon sticks. Pour liquid over pears and chill at least one hour. (You can chill overnight.)

CUSTARD SAUCE:
Combine all ingredients in 4 cup glass measuring cup. Microwave on high for 5-8 minutes until it coats back of a spoon, stirring once or twice during cooking. Chill. (It will thicken after cooling.)

To serve: Place 2 pear quarters in a sauce dish. Add custard sauce. Drizzle with strawberry jam.

Rates at Ty-Bach range from $45-$60, which include a full breakfast.

Victorian Garden Bed and Breakfast

1720 16th Street, Monroe, WI 53566
608•328•1720

Hostess: Marti Cutler

The Victorian Garden Bed and Breakfast is like a tapestry of many different threads. The appeal begins as you turn the corner and catch a glimpse of graceful refinement: gardens alive with color, 100 year old trees framing the brick walkway, and an elegant Victorian beauty that beckons you to climb the porch steps and settle in for a time. The beauty of our home is woven throughout: antique quilts, butternut and fur woodwork, whisps of the past blended with touches of today. The common thread is one of welcome and warmth. Please come visit us soon.

Kay's Blueberry Buckle

serves 9

Ingredients:

3/4 cup sugar
1/4 cup butter
1 egg
1/2 cup milk
2 cups sifted flour
3/4 teaspoon salt
2 teaspoons baking powder
2 cups fresh blueberries

TOPPING:
1/2 cup sugar
1/3 cup flour
1 teaspoon cinnamon
1/4 cup melted butter

Procedure:

Cream butter and sugar; beat in egg, milk. Then sift dry ingredients. Stir in berries. Pour into 9" x 13" pan.
Combine topping ingredients. Mix until crumbly. Sprinkle on blueberry mixture.
Bake 35-40 minutes at 350°. Terrific topped with yogurt, sour cream or whipped cream!

This was a favorite "summertime" recipe of my mom's. I'm sure she'd be pleased at my guests' reaction!

Rates at Victorian Garden range from $45-$150, which include a full or continental breakfast.

Victoria-On-Main Bed and Breakfast

622 W. Main Street (Hwy 12), Whitewater, WI 53190
414•473•8400

Hostess: Nancy Wendt

Come and enjoy our 1895 Victorian home. My specialty is fine cotton linen (which is line dried when possible), down comforters, light and airy rooms (Laura Ashley wallpapers and material), lace curtains, and antiques. Each room features a different wood. The sitting room, kitchen, and wrap-a-round porch are also for your use.

A full breakfast will start your day. Then enjoy the hiking and biking trails, Indian Mounds Park, swimming at Whitewater Lake, or University of Wisconsin-Whitewater across the street, to name a few.

A guest from England wrote to me and said that I had "restored his faith in American hospitality. That's what a bed and breakfast is all about!"

Overnight Caramel French Toast

serves 6

Ingredients:

1 cup packed brown sugar
1/2 cup butter
2 tablespoons light corn syrup
12 slices sandwich bread
6 eggs, beaten
1 1/2 cups milk
1 teaspoon vanilla extract
1/4 teaspoon salt

Procedure:

Combine sugar, butter and corn syrup in a small saucepan, cook over medium heat until thickened, stirring constantly. Pour syrup mixture into a 9" x 13" baking dish. Place 6 slices of bread on top of syrup mixture. Top with remaining 6 slices of bread.

Combine eggs, milk, vanilla and salt, stirring until blended. Pour egg mixture evenly over bread slices. Cover and chill 8 hours or overnight. Bake uncovered at 350° for 40-45 minutes or until lightly browned.

Rates at Victoria-On-Main range from $48-$75, which include a full breakfast.

Victorian Swan on Water

1716 Water Street, Stevens Point, WI 54481
715•345•0595

Hostess: Joan Ouellette

My brother, Chuck Egle, told me he'd be my partner if I located my bed and breakfast in Stevens Point. He also found this great 1889 house and helped restore it to the beauty it once was. It lost a third story and some marble bathtubs in the passing decades but we found the blueprints and it is now a place where history and comfort meet.

It has been a wonderful move for me. This city has everything including a great location. We are just hours away from any part of the state and minutes away from water, a historic downtown, golf, bike and ski trails, birdwatching and the university.

We invite you to enjoy the house, with its plant-filled breakfast room and large light rooms full of antique furnishings, ornate ceiling moldings and inlaid floors. Summer provides lush gardens and in winter, a cozy fireplace and lots of room for reading or games makes this a perfect place to relax.

Frosti Crepes

makes about 28

Ingredients:

1 pound hot pork sausage
1 pound regular pork sausage
1/4 to 1/2 cup chopped onion
1/2 teaspoon marjoram
1/3 cup sour cream
8 ounces cream cheese
1 cup shredded cheddar cheese

BLENDER CREPES:
 (need 2 batches)
1 cup milk
1 cup water
4 medium eggs
2 cups flour
1/2 teaspoon salt
1/4 cup melted butter

TOPPING:
1/2 cup sour cream
Shredded cheese

Procedure:

Crumble sausage and fry. Add onion the last few minutes. Drain fat and add the next 4 ingredients. Mix and set aside while you make 2 batches of crepes.

CREPES:
Combine in blender and mix for 1 minute. Pour about 1/4 cup into oiled 8" skillet, rotating quickly to spread batter. Cook over high heat for about 1 minute—turn and cook just briefly and turn out on tea towel. Separate with wax paper. Makes about 12-14 crepes.

Place about 2 tablespoons of mixture in a crepe, roll up and place in two 9" x 13" baking dishes. Cover and bake 375° 15 minutes or until thoroughly heated. Put sour cream and a sprinkling of cheese across the center of the crepes and bake uncovered for another 5 to 10 minutes.

These may be made the night before and refrigerated or they may be frozen but be sure to increase the baking time. I bake them about 30-40 minutes. I find Jimmy Dean sausage to be the best tasting.

Rates at Victorian Swan range from $45-$65, which include a full breakfast.

Victorian Treasure
Bed and Breakfast Inn

115 Prairie Street, Lodi, WI 53555
608•592•5199; 800•859•5199

Hosts: Kimberly and Todd Seidl

The Victorian Treasure is an apt name for an 1897 Queen Anne that has been lovingly restored and features many original architectural details. At the Victorian Treasure you will be served herbal tea and a sweet before you retire to your turned down bed, and start your day with a full breakfast in the formal dining room. The inn has four unique guest rooms with timeless ambiance and thoughtful amenities—private baths, turndown service, down comforters, terry robes. Double whirlpool bath and an outdoor hot tub are available. Kimberly and Todd have backgrounds in hotel and restaurant management, and provide the friendly and gracious hospitality of a classic bed and breakfast inn.

Elegant Eggs Florentine

serves 8

Ingredients:

MORNAY SAUCE:
   (makes 1 quart)
1/2 cup butter
1/2 cup flour
1/4 cup onion, minced
1 quart cream (or milk)
Salt
White pepper
Red (cayenne) pepper
4 ounces parmesan cheese

8 ounces fresh spinach,
   cleaned and torn (no stems)
1 teaspoon butter
2 medium fresh tomatoes
1 ounce parmesan cheese
12 fresh eggs
1/2 cup cream (or milk)
Small bunch fresh chives
8 English muffins
Butter

Procedure:

This recipe is quite simple . . . just a lot of little steps!

To prepare mornay sauce, melt butter in medium saucepan. Saute onion until clear, add flour (to form a roux), and cook slightly—but do not brown. Slowly add cream (milk is good, but less rich), stirring constantly—no lumps! Season with salt, white pepper, and a dash of red pepper. Cook over low heat 20-30 minutes. Stir in parmesan cheese. (Chef's note: Classic Mornay uses an egg yolk liaison, we choose to omit this step because this rich sauce is used in an egg entree.)

Melt teaspoon of butter in medium frying pan, saute spinach until soft. Set aside.

Slice the tomatoes into 16 even slices, place on cookie sheet, sprinkle with parmesan cheese.

Whip eggs with cream (or milk). Melt butter in a large frying pan, cook eggs over low heat until thoroughly cooked, yet soft. (Gently fold eggs while cooking, do not "over scramble".) Cut 16 pretty ends of chives, about 3-4 inches long, reserve for garnish. Cut remaining into small pieces, add to eggs. Add 2 cups mornay sauce. Hold over very low heat until final assembly.

Toast and butter English muffin halves. Broil tomato slices until slightly browned. Add 1 1/2 cups mornay sauce to spinach. Assemble: Place two English muffin halves on plate. Top with a tomato slice on each muffin. Ladle spinach over both muffin halves, top with egg. Ladle with 2-3 tablespoons mornay sauce over egg, garnish with two chive stems.

Lodging rates at the Victorian Treasure range from $65-$110, which include a full breakfast.

The Whistling Swan

P.O. Box 193, Fish Creek, WI 54212
414•868•3442

Hosts: Jan and Andy Coulson

Entering the historic Whistling Swan in Fish Creek, one half expects to see the aristocratic founder Dr. Herman Welcker, walking briskly down the open staircase, spats neatly buttoned, celluloid collar intact and gloves in hand, shouting "Croquet, anyone?"

Since acquiring the inn in 1985, Jan and Andy Coulson have restored it to its original splendor of 1907, when Dr. Welcker moved it from Marinette, Wisconsin, across the frozen waters of Green Bay.

The spacious and high-ceilinged lobby sets the inn's tone with a white mantled fireplace, arched bay windows and the original restored baby grand piano, at which Dr. Welcker's wife, Henriette, once entertained her guests. Upstairs, guests revel in one of seven meticulously decorated rooms and suites, all with private bathrooms, and each decorated with coordinated wallpapers and fabrics. Antique carved beds and dressers add to the elegant, yet comfortable decor.

Breakfast consists of fresh bakery and fruit, fresh squeezed juice, ground coffee and daily hot specialties, served in the summer on a wide veranda, with its original wicker furniture and splendid view of the historic part of Fish Creek.

Italian Sausage Breakfast Casserole

serves 6

Ingredients:

1/2 cup butter
1/2 pound fresh mushrooms, sliced
1 1/4 cups thinly sliced yellow onions
1 1/2 pounds mild Italian sausage
12 slices buttered bread, crusts removed
2 cups shredded cheddar cheese
5 eggs
2 cups milk
3 teaspoons Dijon mustard
1 teaspoon dry mustard
1/2 teaspoon nutmeg
1/2 teaspoon salt
1/2 teaspoon pepper
2 tablespoons chopped parsley

Procedure:

Grease a 9" x 13" casserole. In a skillet melt the butter and brown the mushrooms and onions until tender, 6-8 minutes. Set aside. Cook the sausage and cut into pieces. In the greased casserole place 6 slices bread, half of mushrooms mixture, half of sausage, and half of the cheese. Repeat the layers ending with cheese. Mix together the eggs, milk, mustards, nutmeg, salt and pepper. Pour over the casserole. Cover and refrigerate overnight. When ready to bake, sprinkle parsley on top and bake uncovered in a 350° oven for 1 hour. Serve immediately.

Rates at the Whistling Swan range from $95-$118 per night for rooms; and $124 per night for suites. Full breakfast included.

Whitefish Bay Farm

3831 Clark Lake Road, Sturgeon Bay, WI 54235
414•743•1560

Hosts: Dick and Gretchen Regnery

Visit Whitefish Bay Farm where the past meets the present. Here, in a 1908 restored American Foursquare farmhouse, you will find four comfortable guest rooms with private baths. Experience the changing view from our dining room where guests gather to share conversation and enjoy an abundant homemade country breakfast. Visit with our registered white and naturally colored Corriedale sheep, see handweaving and handspinning demonstrations in our small art gallery, or relax in the country quiet.

Our farm is located next to Whitefish Dunes State Park where guests are able to enjoy the sand beach and over nine miles of hiking or cross-country ski trails. We are open year around and welcome guests to the quiet side of Door County.

Sour Cream Cherry Pancakes

serves 4-6

Ingredients:

2 cups sifted flour
4 tablespoons sugar
4 teaspoons baking powder
2 eggs, beaten
1 1/2 cups milk
1 cup sour cream (not "lite" sour cream)
6 tablespoons melted margarine or butter
2 cups fresh or frozen Door County red cherries, pitted and halved

Procedure:

Combine flour, sugar and baking powder. Sift into bowl. Combine eggs, milk, sour cream and margarine and stir until smooth. Add dry ingredients and beat until just smooth. Fold in cherries. Bake on lightly greased griddle until done. Serve with butter and maple syrup.

I always use real sour cream and unsalted butter. These pancakes are light and delicious and a favorite of returning guests.

Rates at the Whitefish Bay Farm range from $60-$75, which include full country breakfast

The White Shutters

W265 County Trunk H, Lomira, WI 53048
414•269•4056

Hosts: Rollie Glass and Lorna Schwingle-Glass

The White Shutters offers a relaxed, peaceful country setting. Family heirlooms—furniture and dishes—will make you feel at home in a cozy, informal atmosphere. The rural view from our hilltop location is worth the trip! Our friendly dogs are waiting to take you for a walk.

We are located midway between the Horicon National Wildlife Refuge and the Kettle Moraine State Forest (northern unit).

Many of the recipes used at The White Shutters were acquired from relatives and friends. We thank them for sharing their special recipes with us and you! Poppy Seed Bread has become a favorite to serve for breakfast.

Poppy Seed Bread

2 loaves

Ingredients:

BREAD:
3 cups flour
1 1/2 teaspoons salt
1 1/2 cups milk
2 1/4 cups sugar
1 1/2 teaspoons butter flavoring
1 1/2 teaspoons almond extract
1 1/2 teaspoons baking powder
3 eggs
1 1/8 cups cooking oil
1 1/2 tablespoons poppy seeds

GLAZE:
1/2 teaspoon butter flavoring
1/2 teaspoon almond extract
1/2 teaspoon vanilla
1/4 cup orange juice
3/4 cup sugar

Procedure:

Combine all bread ingredients except the poppy seeds and beat together until well mixed and smooth. Gently stir in poppy seeds. Bake in 2 well-buttered bread pans or 3 small pans or muffins. Bake at 350° for 1 hour—less time if making small loaves.

Combine glaze ingredients in small sauce pan and heat until sugar dissolves. Pour the glaze over baked loaves while the bread is still warm and in the baking pans. Remove from the pans and cool completely.

Rates at The White Shutters range from $35-$60 per night, which include a continental breakfast.

Wolf River Lodge

Star Route, White Lake, WI 54491
715•882•2182

Hosts: Joe and Joan Jesse

One of Wisconsin's great historic country inns overlooking the Wolf River. Comfortable log building. Handmade quilts and braided rugs add warmth to eight antique-filled guest rooms. Full breakfast, restaurant (reservation only), and pub. Written about and praised by state and national publications. Visited by many prominent persons. An ideal hideaway setting for honeymoons, anniversaries, reunions, prom and rehearsal dinners and corporate conferences. Open year round.

Crepe Suzette

10 pancakes

Ingredients:

3 eggs
1 teaspoon salt
1 tablespoon oil
1 cup flour
1 1/2 cups milk
1 tablespoon oil
Strawberry jam
Powdered sugar

Procedure:

Beat first four ingredients with half of the milk until smooth. Add remaining milk. Heat 8" heavy fry pan with sloping sides (or crepe pan) on high heat.

Coat bottom of pan with 1 tablespoon oil. Pour off excess oil. Coat bottom of pan with about 1/3 cup of crepe batter. Fry one side until lightly browned. Flip pancake and cook about 30 seconds. Remove from pan and keep warm. Repeat process to make additional pancakes.

Spread each pancake with homemade strawberry jam. Roll up and sprinkle with powdered sugar.

We serve one crepe in place of toast along with one egg, bacon and country fried potatoes.

Rates at the Wolf River Lodge range from $35-$45, which include a full breakfast.

The Wooden Heart Inn

11086 Highway 42, Sister Bay, WI 54234
414•854•9451

Hosts: Mike and Marilyn Hagerman

We welcome you to our newly-constructed log home nestled in the woods on the north side of Sister Bay in Door County, Wisconsin. It combines the charm of an old home with modern amenities and is furnished with meticulously-restored antiques. Our guests are welcome to use the great room and to join us each evening for refreshments by the large stone fireplace.

Guests are served a full country breakfast on a 180-piece set of handpainted Bavarian china dating to 1890.

The three guest rooms are located on the second floor along with a loft where guests may watch TV, play games or read. Each room has a queen-sized bed and a small private bath with shower. The rooms are decorated in themes—apples, cherries and hearts.

There is a gift shop specializing in Scandinavian gifts located off the great room—called "The Back Porch."

One of our guests wrote to us, "The Wooden Heart Inn is a very welcome addition to the world of bed and breakfast. We give a four-heart rating to your inn."

Baked Stuffed Pears

serves 8

Ingredients:

8 pears (ripe but firm)

FILLING:
1/2 cup raisins (golden)
1/4 cup chopped nuts (walnuts or pecans)
3 tablespoons sugar
1 1/2 tablespoons lemon juice

SYRUP:
1/2 cup water
1/2 cup light corn syrup
1 tablespoon cinnamon red-hot candies

Procedure:

    Peel the pears. Leave the stems on. Core the pear from the bottom. Combine the filling ingredients in a small bowl, mixing well. Divide the filling equally among the 8 pears. Place the pears upright in a deep covered baking dish. Mix the syrup ingredients and pour into the baking dish. Bake in a preheated, 350° oven for approximately 1 hour and 15 minutes, basting occasionally. Pears are done when easily pierced with a fork. Spoon syrup over the pears. Can be served warm or cold.

We serve these in a beautiful footed compote dish along with "mini" muffins or tiny home-baked ginger snaps. The pears are served before the hot entree. We believe that how you serve a dish like this is almost as important as what you serve.

Rates at The Wooden Heart Inn range from $75-$85 per night, which include a full breakfast.

Yankee Hill Bed and Breakfast

405 Collins Street, Plymouth, WI 53073
414•892•2222

Hosts: Jim and Peg Stahlman

We welcome you into the ambiance of quiet, small town life in the heart of the scenic Kettle Moraine recreational area. We offer two historic homes. One is an 1891 Queen Anne home which is a Sheboygan County Landmark. The other, an 1870 Gothic Italianate, is listed on the National Register of Historic Places. These homes were built in the "Yankee Hill" area of Plymouth by two hard working, affluent brothers— Henry and Gilbert Huson. These brothers valued craftmanship and lasting quality. Their values are still honored here. These homes are furnished with period antiques. You'll enjoy the short drive to Wade House, Kettle Moraine recreational area, Road America, the Old Plank Road recreational trail, antiquing, and excellent restaurants. Choose one of our eleven guest rooms, six of which have a private bath. Some with whirlpools. Relaxation comes easily in this atmosphere as you stroll the pleasant one acre property. Older children welcome.
Gift Certificates Available!

Chocolate Tea Bread

Makes 1 - 9" x 5" loaf

Ingredients:

1 1/2 cups flour
1 1/3 cups sugar
1/3 cup cocoa
1 teaspoon baking soda
3/4 teaspoon salt
1/4 teaspoon baking powder
1/3 cup softened margarine or shortening
2 eggs
1/2 cup applesauce
1/3 cup water
1/3 cup chocolate chips
1/3 cup chopped nuts

Procedure:

In a large bowl combine first ten ingredients. Stir together. Beat 30 seconds with electric mixer on low speed, then 3 minutes on high speed. Stir in chips and nuts. Pour into greased and floured 9" x 5" loaf pan. Bake at 350° for 1 hour. Cool 5 minutes in pan. Turn out on wire rack to finish cooling.

Rates at Yankee Hill range from $61-$93. Rates include a full breakfast.

Ye Olde Manor House Bed and Breakfast

Rural Route 5, Box 390 Route 12/67, Elkhorn, WI 53121
414•742•2450

Hosts: Babette and Marvin Henschel

Our early 20th century Manor House, filled with both antiques and comfortable furniture and set on three spacious wooded acres, is the perfect place to relax—forget your cares and worries—even if only for a day or two. When you leave, you'll be refreshed and ready to meet the world.

We try to join our guests for breakfast, and we find the ambiance at our table is marvelous. People who are strangers the night before develop exciting conversations. That, along with a delicious breakfast, keeps our guests coming back.

Babs' Philly Cinnamon Buns

serves 12

Ingredients:

2 packages Pillsbury Crescent rolls
5 tablespoons margarine (or butter) melted
3/4 cup brown sugar

2 teaspoons cinnamon (divided)
1/3 cup dark Karo syrup
1/3 cup raisins
1/3 cup chopped walnuts or pecans

Procedure:

Can be baked in a 10" x 2" round cake pan or in a muffin tin, and served as schnecken.

Spray pan with vegetable spray. If using large cake pan melt margarine in it. Heat oven to 375°. Open both packages of rolls and lay out, sides touching on counter. Press flat to close holes and spoon melted margarine all over. Sprinkle 1 teaspoon cinnamon on dough and other in pan. Sprinkle half brown sugar on dough and rest in pan. Sprinkle raisins and nuts on dough. Pour syrup in pan and stir well to blend glaze.

Roll up filled dough, and using a serrated knife cut into 12 equal slices. Lay slices cut side up in pan. There is space between, but as it rises in oven it joins together. Bake for 30 minutes. If not nicely browned, give an extra few minutes. Have plate ready and as soon as you remove it from oven, place plate on top and invert.

For individual buns, melt margarine in a small saucepan, Spread it on dough, then add remainder of cinnamon, sugar and syrup to pan. Spoon about a tablespoon of glaze into muffin tins sprayed with non-stick cooking spray, and place dough cut side up on top of glaze. Bake 15 minutes or until brown. Place waxed paper on counter, and when buns are ready, invert on it.

Great taste . . .

This delicious breakfast cake is best made the day you want to serve it. I made shortcuts and it takes only 45 minutes from start to finish.

Rates at Ye Olde Manor House range from $40-$80, which include a full breakfast.

To order additional copies send $12.50 to:

Barry Luce
The Fargo Mansion Inn
406 Mulberry Street
Lake Mills, WI 53551
(price includes all handling fees)

Name _____

Address _____

City _____ State _____ Zip _____

Cookbooks make great gifts!

....

To order a W.B.B.H.H.I.A. Directory
send your request to:

Barry Luce
The Fargo Mansion Inn
406 Mulberry Street
Lake Mills, WI 53551

Name _____

Address _____

City _____ State _____ Zip _____

Thank you for your support of
Wisconsin Bed and Breakfast Homes and Historic Inns Association.

To order additional copies send $12.50 to:

Barry Luce
The Fargo Mansion Inn
406 Mulberry Street
Lake Mills, WI 53551
(price includes all handling fees)

Name _____

Address _____

City _____ State _____ Zip _____

Cookbooks make great gifts!

....

To order a W.B.B.H.H.I.A. Directory
send your request to:

Barry Luce
The Fargo Mansion Inn
406 Mulberry Street
Lake Mills, WI 53551

Name _____

Address _____

City _____ State _____ Zip _____

Thank you for your support of
Wisconsin Bed and Breakfast Homes and Historic Inns Association.